A Brilliant IQ
Gift or Challenge?

Lyn Kendall and Chris Allcock

Acknowledgements

I am not a genius. The contents of this book didn't just pop into my head. They are the culmination of a lifetime's experience as a gifted child, mother to an exceptionally able son, a teacher and psychologist. Thanks are due to so many people so if you have ever taught me, worked with me, lived with me or been my friend, thank you. You are all my teachers.

I do want to name a few names. My parents, Barbara and Ken, and step-parents, Reg and Viv, for finding endless ways of keeping this inquisitive child busy and being patient with a difficult teen. My form tutor Mr. Haynes, who persuaded me to stay on at school and take my exams. The late Victor Serebriakoff, my friend and mentor, who showed me anything is possible if you have the confidence to go for it. Lu Alsop and Suzette Gillman, colleagues who helped me design and refine new ways of working with children and young people.

John Stevenage, Ann Clarkson, Bobby Raikhy and the staff at the Mensa office for unending support. Tina Crawford, Abbie Robson and Sarah Reid, parents of bright sparks who have provided undying support for me. My husband Colin, not only for his love and support but for providing me with words when I had brain freeze. Finally, to my son Chris. Thank you for showing me that it is possible to follow a dream and thank you for having enough faith in me to co-write this book. I have learned so much from you.

Lyn

Published by
Brilliant Publications Limited
Unit 10
Sparrow Hall Farm
Edlesborough
Dunstable
Bedfordshire
LU6 2ES, UK

www.brilliantpublications.co.uk

The name Brilliant Publications and the logo are registered trademarks.

Written by Lyn Kendall and Chris Allcock

© Brilliant Publications Limited 2020

Printed ISBN: 9780857478344
ePDF ISBN: 9780857478368

First printed and published in 2020

Printed and bound by:
Ashford Colour Press Ltd, Gosport, Hants
PO13 0FW

Contents

About the Authors

Lyn Kendall is a psychologist and educator who serves as British Mensa's Gifted Child Consultant. She has over 40 years' experience working with children of all ages and intellects, focusing mainly on the fields of Special Educational Needs and Gifted and Talented Education. Lyn holds a Master's Degree in Education (Special Needs and Inclusive Education), an Advanced Diploma in Special Needs in Education and is both a qualified psychologist and a member of the British Psychological Society.

Lyn was inspired to join Mensa in 1988 after completing a puzzle in one of its advertisements. While attending her first Annual General Meeting for the society she met Victor Serebriakoff, then President of Mensa, who became a friend and mentor. Victor encouraged Lyn to pursue her ambition to offer care and guidance for those who live or work with gifted children.

Now appointed as Mensa's Gifted Child Consultant, Lyn provides advice and support for parents and professionals alike, as well as undertaking media work for programmes like Victoria Derbyshire and This Morning. She appears regularly on Channel 4's hit TV show Child Genius, where she collaborates with the production team behind the scenes as well as being a panellist.

As part of a career spent aiding and encouraging all aspects of Gifted and Talented Education, Lyn's other activities include lecturing at universities, giving media interviews, advising Local Education Authorities, creating teaching materials for Gifted and Talented Coordinators, running workshops and facilitating summer schools for children of all ages.

Lyn retired from full-time teaching in 2017 to focus on her private consultancy work, and now provides assessment and support services under the banner of Kendall Tuition, in addition to producing information packs and resources for parents of intellectually able youngsters. She tours the United Kingdom to deliver her signature talks designed to help parents, teachers and psychologists live and work with gifted children.

Lyn lives in the Midlands with her husband Colin and their cats. In her spare time she plays competitive Scrabble and is a member of the Association of British Scrabble Players. She also enjoys music, reading, cooking, knitting and making jewellery. She has been a keen player of computer and video games since the day she bought her son his first Nintendo system.

Chris Allcock is a professional writer and games designer with more than 15 years' experience in the video game industry. As an experienced writer, he has collaborated with other creative professionals to create multiple forms of media including video game scripts and stories, strategy guides, art books, comics, audio dramas, promotional materials and more.

Chris's print portfolio includes several video game tie-in works such as _The Art of Sea of Thieves_, _The Art of Borderlands 3_ and _Sea of Thieves: Athena's Fortune_. His non-fiction work includes multiple reviews and features for the popular UK culture site Den of Geek.

Having joined Mensa at the age of seven, co-authoring A Brilliant IQ has presented Chris an opportunity to offer the perspective of someone who overcame many of the same challenges, and reassure bright sparks everywhere that they have what it takes to thrive."

He currently resides in the Midlands and is probably drinking tea.

Note: Because this book is based on Lyn's many years of experience of working with gifted children and their parents, the authors have chosen to use the first person when writing the book.

Preface

For many years, I've toured the UK giving a number of different talks on the subject of gifted children to interested groups of parents, teachers and psychologists. The content of these talks varies slightly depending upon the audience I'm talking to, but the core points I make are always the same, and this book can be thought of as a vastly expanded version of everything I cover in those seminars. (You'll have to provide your own tea and biscuits, though!)

Although I hope that its contents will be of interest to psychologists, it's important to note that this book is not a piece of psychological research, nor is it a 'quick-fix' manual – there's no such thing! That said, it's my hope that anyone who reads it will come to appreciate the unique hurdles our bright sparks face as they move through the world around them, and that they'll refer back to particular sections if and when the need arises. Many chapters also contain activities that are designed to help us see things from other people's points of view, rather than focusing on our own perspectives.

We'll begin by looking briefly at the history of IQ testing and how we even go about defining a highly intelligent child, then we'll look at both the advantages and unique challenges – physical, social and emotional issues – that can affect our bright sparks throughout their lives.

In the second half of the book, I'll outline what I call my 'Four Rules for Success', explaining how I developed them and why they can help bright sparks to manage their extraordinary intellects and overcome life's obstacles. We'll also discuss how parents and teachers can offer help and support, both at home and when our gifted youngsters head to school.

Finally, I've provided a list of recommended reading and other useful resources, as well as ways to contact me in person if you suspect you might have a bright spark of your own. Whatever your reasons for picking up this book, I sincerely hope it will be not just informative, but also help to reassure both gifted children and their parents that they are far from alone.

Introduction

I was born a square peg. As adults, there are times when we all know the feeling of struggling to fit into a round hole that simply wasn't designed to contain us. Perhaps we feel it when we're trying to make conversation at a party packed with strangers who all know one another, or if we find ourselves bored senseless by the latest craze that has everyone else enthralled.

When I was growing up, though, I never once realised just how much of a square peg I was. I certainly never imagined that the reason for my differences was that I was classed as a 'gifted child'. I considered myself odd, yes, but otherwise ordinary.

What I did know is that, when I was young, I was the one that the other children would come to when they were bored, so that I could think up games and activities for them. As I moved through school, I was often sent to help my classmates with their reading. When I was old enough, I unwittingly began to tutor the first of many square pegs to come – my younger cousin David.

Even when he was a baby, I could see that David was bored. My relatives would tell me that he cried a lot and I would suggest giving him something to do, as it was obvious to me that he was looking around in search of stimulation. I would crumple up a ball of paper so he could explore its texture and malleability with pudgy little hands. Once he'd learned to talk, he would tell me with great enthusiasm about the inventions and machines he was designing in his mind.

Shortly after school began, David started refusing to read. When I arrived to babysit I'd find the books the school had sent home lying untouched on the table – in hindsight, I suspect this refusal stemmed from boredom, as he already knew how to read them perfectly well. Instead, we'd read the books backwards, or read across both pages at once, playing with the words themselves to make them fun again. In a way, David was my first gifted student.

I'd drifted naturally towards teaching during my sixth-form years, having already taken a group of 'difficult' teens on a camping trip and secured my own cupboard at a nearby secondary school where I would help the students learn to read. It was at my first teaching placement, though, that I really understood my natural affinity for square pegs.

Rather than being thrown in at the deep end as they are nowadays, it was common for teachers-in-training to spend time at a primary school and work with a small group under the supervision of the teacher. The day after I arrived, the teacher I was assigned to was taken ill. (I'm reasonably sure it wasn't my fault!) Since I was available, the school decided not to hire a substitute teacher and gave me a teaching assistant instead. This left me in charge of an entire class of children, one of whom was a boy named Rupert.

Rupert was exceptionally bright and had both an undying love for, and an extensive knowledge of, dinosaurs and space. Soon he was sucking in information as fast as I could relay it and standing up in front of the other children to talk about the planets. Had I been a more experienced teacher I would have given more time to the other children who maybe weren't ready for this type of learning, but I found being able to stimulate and challenge Rupert utterly delightful. When my placement was over, Rupert and his family gifted me a book which I still treasure to this day.

The book gifted to Lyn by Rupert and his family.

Having finally realised that I was most interested in working with children who landed at either end of the ability spectrum, I was fortunate that my first teaching position was in the Solihull Borough, home to one of the first ever Special Educational Needs programmes in the UK. This also included gifted children and it was with their support that I first trained in Cognitive

Behavioural Therapy, learned how to administer tests and honed many more skills I've relied upon all my professional life.

This book represents a distillation: everything I have learned during a career borne from that first position. It draws from four decades of classroom experience, from my colleagues in education, inspiring teachers, family and parenthood, contacts made during my work with British Mensa and the countless children, parents and caregivers who have come to see me for consultation and advice over the years. It also elaborates upon the central themes and messages of my seminars and workshops.

Above all else, I hope that this book helps to reassure parents who know, or suspect they know, that they have a gifted child living under their roof. There may be many unusual challenges ahead, and not every day will be a good day. Being possessed of high intelligence hands neither the child nor their parent a golden ticket to life's chocolate factory.

Happily, it is equally true that there are ways to mitigate those issues, to raise a balanced, well-rounded human being and lay the groundwork so that everyone in the family can enjoy a contented life together. There are many moments of joy to be found while raising our square pegs, regardless what shape of hole they eventually choose to make their own.

Chapter 1

What it Means to Have a High IQ

Chapter 1:
What it Means to Have a High IQ

Bright sparks, whiz kids, wunderkind... There's been no shortage of ways dreamed up to refer to intelligent people over the years, so let's begin by defining the concepts at the very heart of this book: what is intelligence, and how might we classify it? What makes one person 'gifted', but not another?

Considered scientifically, intelligence is raw brainpower as it applies to:

- Problem-solving – the ability to grasp the nature of an obstacle or dilemma and to think a way through or around the issue. (Green and Gilhooly 2010)

- Speed of processing – how quickly information can be taken in, assimilated and recalled.

- Attention – how much input can be usefully taken in at any time, and the level of detail recorded. (Naish 2010; Ness 2010)

- Working Memory – how much information can be actively retained and manipulated at any one time. (Hitch 2010)

These aspects of intelligence are innate and with us from the moment we're born; they are affected by our genes and our in-utero development. After we're born, our intelligence can be honed with practice and development, and occasionally stunted if some unfortunate trauma occurs or some other condition, such as Alzheimer's Disease, manifests. Our intelligence also diminishes slightly as we age.

Are we, as a species, more intelligent than we used to be? Our distant ancestors, like the 'caveman' pictured on the next page, are often portrayed as being less intellectually able than we are today. In fact, those ancestors would have been struggling to survive on a day-to-day basis. Hunger, predation, disease, exposure to harsh climate and the threat of attack from others – all of these perils would have taken their toll on the population and our forebears' intelligence would have been channelled into dealing with them.

It would have been our most intelligent ancestors who learned to harness and control fire, to craft tools and weapons and understand what made them effective, and to use the pelts of animals to stay warm. Even today, we can see examples of intelligence being used to tackle the problems of survival. When, for example, young children in remote tribes become accomplished physicians, they have channelled their intellect where it's needed the most.

Where and when you were born does not have any impact on your intelligence, nor is intellect the purview of the middle or upper classes. Wealth and cultural background have no part to play in the potential we are born with. That said, how well we make use of that intelligence often depends on our temperament and how we are educated.

We receive that education from all sorts of places, not just school or other academic programmes. From the moment we arrive in the world we are surrounded by people, culture and an environment that contribute to everything we learn. Post-birth, our brains continue to grow and we absorb everything at an amazing rate, assimilating all the information we need to function within our family and the world around us.

Appropriate body language, physical contact, responding to those around us, dangers, comfort sources, relationships, language, concepts of property, social hierarchy – we are invisibly educated in all of these things as we grow. Formal education for some (but certainly not all) of us follows much later.

The more we learn about brain development, the more we come to understand that academic performance is just one facet of our intelligence. If intellect, then, is more than classroom learning and book-smarts, how do we define a highly intelligent individual when considered against their peers, particularly children? What classifies a 'gifted' child?

(As a side-note, I personally dislike the term 'gifted' as it describes an attribute that has been bestowed upon a person rather than their innate ability. I prefer the term 'exceptionally able' and often refer to intelligent children as 'bright sparks' – however, the term 'gifted' is a common frame of reference, and will sometimes be used within this book. The catch-all term 'gifted and talented' only adds to the confusion, so we shall take 'gifted' to mean those individuals with a high intellectual ability who excel across many domains, while 'talented' refers to those who possess a particular aptitude in a single area, such as art, technology or sport.)

In truth, the definition of a gifted individual has changed many times over the years, and will doubtlessly continue to do so as we learn more about our brains and ourselves. Generally speaking, for adults, organizations like Mensa aver that having an IQ that falls within the top 2% of the population classifies an individual as gifted. Some IQ tests also choose to use the term 'gifted' as part of their own classifications.

With children, the question becomes even more complicated. A few minutes spent online reveals a plethora of different figures, competing terminology and a host of definitions, few if any of which agree. While Mensa accepts children whose IQ falls into the top 2% on a standardised test, schools and other bodies in the UK look to the Government for guidance on the matter. They are frequently disappointed.

Over the years, gifted children have: been ignored entirely, been classed as the top 10% of children in any given school in terms of their academic attainment, and conversely described as the top 5% of children in the overall population. More recently, the term 'gifted' has been discarded entirely. 'High attainers', the current term, covers those in the top 25% academically but does not specifically mention giftedness.

Guidance on how schools should accommodate their gifted children has proven to be even more fluid and inconsistent. Previously, schools have been informed that all children are gifted in their own ways, then later that teachers should make their own registers and provisions for Gifted and Talented students. Institutions have been given funding for summer schools, then that funding has been rescinded just as quickly.

Ofsted, the Government office that inspects schools, has in some years made Gifted and Talented provision a focus of its inspections, then grouped those children together with High Attainers. One Ofsted publication, released in 2012, described gifted students as "Pupils who achieved a level 5 or above in both English and mathematics at the end of Year 6." It's clear that someone being gifted means many different things to many different people. In truth, for reasons we will explore later in this book, parents will be well aware that high intelligence and high attainment do not automatically go hand-in-hand.

The definition of giftedness I personally feel most comfortable with was given by HMI (Her Majesty's Inspectorate, who work on behalf of Ofsted among other duties) in 1992, and reads as follows: "A gifted child shows a particular talent or aptitude for learning that is unusual, or considerably beyond, what would normally be expected for that age group." Why this one? Well, while it could be considered a bit woolly, it's not totally focused on attainment and the education system. It allows for the fact that many bright sparks don't always shine in a classroom, and removes the notion of a definitive threshold beyond which a child moves from being 'well above average' to Gifted.

If there's been one relatively consistent thread running throughout all these definitions of giftedness, it's a tendency to rely on results from standardised IQ testing and to group children accordingly. Why, though, do we place such stock in these tests? Where did they come from in the first place, and what makes them a trustworthy tool?

The notion of formal testing for intelligence is more recent than many might suppose. In the 19th century, discussions around the very nature of intellect were considered squarely within the realm of philosophers – the field of psychology itself began as a particular branch of philosophy. It took the efforts of scholars such as William James, often labelled the 'Father of American Psychology', to establish the study of the human mind as a valid science in its own right – and, like any science, it required a series of standards and repeatable experiments in order to be truly rigorous.

It was this movement from discussion and thought experiments towards uniform, quantifiable scales of measurement that laid the groundwork for IQ tests, although their first widespread use was hardly motivated by scientific intent. Standardised tests that focused largely on educational attainment were deployed in the 1930s and 40s as part of armed services training, the intention being to separate out those recruits who could take on more capable positions from those who were to serve as little more than cannon fodder.

Nowadays, IQ tests are generally used for more benign purposes, and while there are many different tests available, the fundamentals are the same: the person taking the test answers a series of questions, generally working within some kind of time constraint, and their answers are awarded marks. Their total number of marks is then checked against that test's scale to deliver their Intelligence Quotient, or IQ.

While they might seem intimidating, IQ tests are constructed very carefully, and aren't designed to trick or confuse their participants in the way that a fiendish brainteaser or cryptic crossword might be. Questions are selected carefully based upon current research and improve upon tests that have come before in an effort to assess as many aspects of intelligence as possible.

Once the questions have been selected, they are taken out and tested in diverse locations such as schools, armed forces installations and old people's homes – places where a large, diverse group of people can be found who are of a similar age to one another. These sample sets are as large as possible, ideally taking in hundreds of thousands of participants.

Chapter 1: What it Means to Have a High IQ

Once the sample results have been collated, the results are plotted and statistical techniques used so that the test can state, with a reasonable level of certainty, how an 'average' person of a particular age might be expected to score on the various questions. While this is going on, the validity and voracity of the questions will be examined, as will the ethics of the test itself – creating a scientifically rigorous IQ test is a huge amount of work across a number of different disciplines, and this explains why the tests can be so expensive to purchase. Part of why psychologists charge what they do for an assessment is to recoup the cost of buying up-to-date tests!

The precise contents of IQ tests are kept confidential, partly to ensure that participants can't skew the results, deliberately or otherwise, by looking the test up ahead of time. Therefore, we will use a selection of original questions created for this book in the example IQ test shown here. They're similar to the kinds of problems you might find in some IQ tests or in the puzzle section of a magazine, and they will prove useful when we think about instances where IQ tests work really well, and a couple of cases where they don't.

The specific answers can be found at the end of this chapter, but consider the types of problem that were posed – there's a heavy emphasis on spotting patterns, spatial awareness and lateral thinking, all of which test intelligence. They're very different questions from the kind you might find in an English exam or a general knowledge quiz,

Connections
1. 'Hot' is to 'cold' as 'top' is to …
2. 'Baby' is to 'adult' as 'chick' is to …
3. 'Trombone' is to 'brass' as 'oboe' is to …

Meanings
4. What is a tree?
5. What is hop?
6. What is sleep?

What comes next?

7. …

8. …

9. Red, dog, girl, lettuce, easy, yellow, …

10. Which net makes the cube?
a. b. c.

11. How many small cubes make up the big cube?

12. I am facing north. I take a turn to my right, then to my left twice, then to my right three times. Which direction am I now facing?

which test your education, and this means IQ tests can offer different insights from, for example, a reading comprehension test.

When I was working in full-time education, I met Simon – an 11-year-old boy who arrived in Year 7 with a label of 'SEN', or Special Educational Needs. At that point, Simon's 'reading age' was 8 years, 6 months, rather than the 11 years that you might expect. Unusually, Simon didn't want to come out of his regular lessons for some extra reading practice – instead I saw him for 15 minutes each morning before school started.

What I noticed about Simon was that his vocabulary was amazing and that he loved to learn. Within a short period his reading age had caught up, but Simon still wanted our time together so that he could read more science books. After speaking to his parents, I referred him to the school's Educational Psychologist (EP), who gave Simon an IQ test. The IQ test showed that rather than being of low ability, Simon was actually in the top 10% of the population. This result encouraged further testing, which revealed that Simon was not only bright, he was also dyslexic. With a proper understanding of Simon's educational needs, he flourished and went on to university.

Unfortunately, the formats of IQ tests present other problems of their own. Angel was a 7-year-old girl with cerebral palsy and hydrocephalus. The muscle constriction in her body was so severe that she couldn't speak. Not being able to talk to her teachers and other children was a source of great frustration for her, so we taught Angel and the other children some basic sign language. Soon Angel was able to sign colours, tell us what she wanted to drink, and convey other more personal needs.

Seeing that Angel had a capacity to learn made me curious. I used a non-verbal IQ test and found that Angel was functioning at a 4-year-old level; clearly well behind her actual age, but beyond what anyone had previously suspected. Next, we began teaching her to read using basic flashcards that could also be used to construct simple sentences – "I am happy", "I am tired" and so on.

Chapter 1: What it Means to Have a High IQ

Shortly before Angel's Annual Review, an EP came to review her functioning. I sat in on the session and explained that Angel could sign some very basic words. What happened next made my heart sink.

"What colour is coal?" asked the EP. Angel looked blank, and I wondered how many other 7-year-olds knew what coal was in the age of central heating. The next question, the colour of snow, was more successful. Angel made the sign for 'white'. I translated, but was informed by the EP that unless Angel delivered the answer verbally, it would be marked as incorrect. Her final score declared that Angel was working at the intellectual level of a 2-year-old.

As well constructed as they are, IQ tests do not present a completely level playing field for those who cannot speak, who are severely visually impaired, or whose primary language differs from the one in which the test is being administered. Consider the third question in our sample IQ test, "Trombone is to brass…" and all of the different circumstances in the life of a living, breathing human being that might prevent them from knowing the English word for one particular musical instrument. Similarly, someone with a particular type of colour blindness might struggle to answer the seventh question.

Online IQ tests, which are freely available on a number of websites, present a few problems of their own. For one thing, they can be repeated multiple times and don't take place under proper test conditions. On the other hand, they also present their own barriers to entry, particularly if the person taking the test finds it difficult to use computer interfaces. Still, these tests can be a fun diversion and may provide a broad assessment of someone's ability that encourages them to undertake a professional IQ test.

By now, you may have noticed that whenever the results of IQ tests have been discussed, we have made reference to someone being in 'the top x% of the population'. Below, we've provided the final scoring charts for two different – and entirely fictitious – IQ tests.

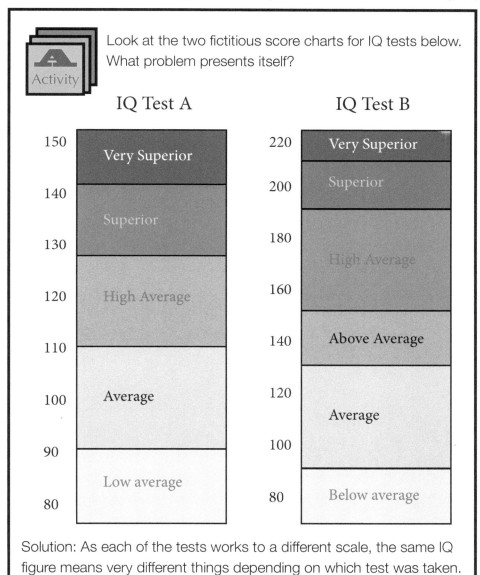

Look at the two fictitious score charts for IQ tests below. What problem presents itself?

IQ Test A

150	Very Superior
140	
130	Superior
120	High Average
110	
100	Average
90	
80	Low average

IQ Test B

220	Very Superior
200	Superior
180	High Average
160	
140	Above Average
120	Average
100	
80	Below average

Solution: As each of the tests works to a different scale, the same IQ figure means very different things depending on which test was taken.

The allure of an IQ that can be represented as a figure, one that can be easily ranked against one's peers, is undeniable. The press in particular love being able to compare, say, Stephen Hawking to Albert Einstein using their respective IQs, never mind that Einstein never took an IQ test in the first place!

The problem, as we can see from the activity on page 19, is that the same number can mean two very different things depending on the test used to define it. That's why, when psychologists talk about intelligence, we place people in percentiles like the 'top 2% qualifier' given by Mensa. The actual number may vary from test to test, but your percentile placement is far more consistent.

The study of intelligence as a psychological science continues to improve as we develop new tools and learn more about our own minds. An IQ test is a valuable tool indeed but, as we have seen, the results are not completely foolproof and should be considered with the proper context, particularly when it comes to comparing numbers. Of course, as many parents will tell you, signs that you have a gifted child manifest themselves long before the time comes to sit them down in front of an IQ test…

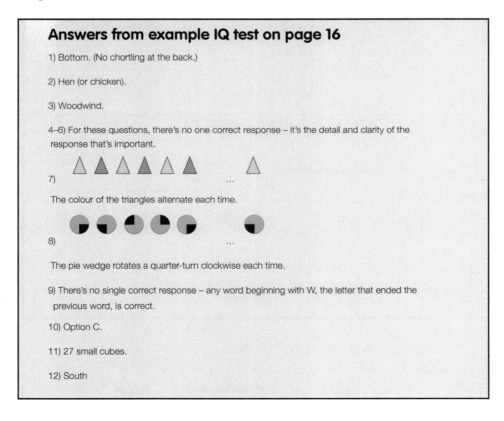

Answers from example IQ test on page 16

1) Bottom. (No chortling at the back.)

2) Hen (or chicken).

3) Woodwind.

4–6) For these questions, there's no one correct response – it's the detail and clarity of the response that's important.

7)

The colour of the triangles alternate each time.

8)

The pie wedge rotates a quarter-turn clockwise each time.

9) There's no single correct response – any word beginning with W, the letter that ended the previous word, is correct.

10) Option C.

11) 27 small cubes.

12) South

Chapter 2

Identifying a Gifted Child

Chapter 2:
Identifying a Gifted Child

What does a gifted child look like? Certain cynical journalists, or the people who write TV sitcoms, would have you believe you can recognise them from their oversized spectacles, pocket calculator and bad haircut. The truth, of course, is that gifted individuals come in all shapes and sizes, from all walks of life, and many will be just as interested in athletics as others are in arithmetic.

This comes as no real surprise, as the forces that shape the person we become have less to do with our intelligence and much more to do with our culture, temperament and how we're raised. Just like our prehistoric ancestors, it's our environment that affects what we consider to be engaging or important. Intelligence doesn't define our interests, although it can enable us to engage with them more deeply.

Likewise, the stereotype that all bright sparks are weedy, physically unimposing people who hate PE and sport in general doesn't hold water. As shown by his post-match conferences, tennis superstar Roger Federer is proficient in half-a-dozen different languages, while the Brazilian footballer known simply as 'Socrates' lived up to his namesake's legacy by receiving a Bachelor's Degree in medicine while simultaneously juggling his sporting career – and still found time to co-found a political movement!

Intelligent people are often highly competitive, so it's no surprise that many find sports and athletics so appealing. Having worked on some of the first IQ tests, American psychologist Lewis Terman embarked on a 35-year longitudinal study, Genetic Studies of Genius (Terman 1959,1989; Hastorf 2016). His study, which began in 1921 and followed children with exceptionally high IQs throughout their lives, confirmed that many of the participants – nicknamed Terman's Termites – did not adhere to the negative stereotypes and many thrived both socially and academically.

Just like everyone else, the personalities of gifted people will change as they move through their lives. My son, for instance, was born a total extrovert. He loved any sort of attention and was a natural entertainer. One Christmas, when he was still small enough to be riding in the seat of a supermarket trolley, we were queueing at the very busy checkouts. He turned to me and said in a loud voice, "Mummy, why are these people so sad? Come on, everyone, it's Christmas!" He proceeded to regale everyone with a selection of Christmas songs for the next 10 minutes, accompanied by anyone brave enough to join in. I wasn't one of them. When he was nine, my son featured in a BBC documentary about gifted children, the results of which caused the BBC to call me and offer him the chance to host his own TV show. I was so excited as I made my way up to his room with the news. His response? "I think I've done enough TV now. Let someone else have a go."

The next few years were marked by dark clothing, hoodies, silence and him barely leaving his room. Computers of various types filled the spaces where books and comics used to be, and he began muttering strange, arcane phrases like 'back-up server'. The man that emerged is a balance between those two previous incarnations. He still loves to entertain, though black clothing continues to dominate his wardrobe.

So – how can you tell? Well, gifted people may not all match a single geeky stereotype, but they do usually have a few unusual traits in common. Let's take a look at 12 of the usual suspects, along with notable examples I've picked up over the years from my own life as well as from parents I've worked with.

1. They have an unusual capacity for remembering things

You may find, when sitting down for story time, that a gifted child is able to quote the text back at you word for word – my son knew several of Roger Hargreaves' *Mr. Men* books off by heart when he was 2 years old. They might also remember routes to places they've only been to once before, song lyrics, conversations or events they were witness to – even the ones you'd prefer they forget – and, of course, can remember the name of every dinosaur that ever existed, not to mention correct you on the ones that don't.

One parent I support has a dinosaur-obsessed 3-year-old named Rowan whose childminder was telling her charges a story while holding a toy brachiosaurus. She ended the story by adding, jokingly, "And then he gobbled us all up!"

"No, he didn't," Rowan admonished her. "He's a herbivore!"

2. They start reading at an early age

Even without any formal teaching, you'll notice bright sparks pointing out road signs or notices in shop windows and telling you what they mean, or recognising words they first saw in a different context. Unwilling to wait for school, it's also possible they'll try to coerce you into teaching them how to read ahead of time, or even try and teach themselves in secret if they fail to do so.

3. They pass intellectual milestones early

As babies and toddlers, they clearly understand what you say to them even before they can talk back. When I was just learning to walk, my mother was taking a bath and realised she'd left her towel in another room. Jokingly, she said to me "Oh no, I've left the bath towel in the bedroom; will you go and fetch it?" She described how shocked she was when I returned after a few minutes, obediently dragging the towel behind me as best I could.

Of course, most parents – particularly first-timers – don't have a baseline to compare against. Often, it'll be other people who spot that your child is ahead of the curve and tell you so, and it's only when you examine developmental checklists you realise that they're right.

4. They have unusual hobbies and in-depth knowledge

Generally, any particular fascinations at a young age will be to do with either nature or science and technology. One young man I worked with could name every brand of car and identify car badges in isolation. Sometimes, however, this level of knowledge can cause distress if it's absorbed without proper context or if the emotional development isn't there to cope with the ramifications of what's been learned. (We'll look at the fallout from this later in the book.)

24

One mother told me about the horrified look on her son's face after watching a documentary about the Big Bang. "So, we're all just made of the things from the periodic table? It can't be. We can't be, we're not droids!" Though it seems like a funny story that would be easily forgotten, the concept continued to terrify him and cause nightmares for nearly a year.

5. They have a developed sense of humour

Bright children love jokes, particularly puns and wordplay, and start to experiment with them from a young age, swiftly passing through the 'knock knock' stage of joke telling. One mother told me how, rather than going to sleep as she should have been, her daughter was racing around her bedroom, the floor of which was covered with scores of books – many of which she was reading concurrently.

As you might expect, this led to a slip, a skid and a bump into the side of the bed. There was no hurt a cuddle couldn't sort out, and afterwards the Mum said light-heartedly, "Who'd have thought a book could be so dangerous?"

"Well," her daughter replied, "the pen is mightier than the sword!"

6. They hold themselves to impossible standards

I know that parents exist who 'hot-house' their children, but a lot of the time, slowing them down is the challenge. There's no tying them to chairs and force-feeding them facts; they're driven, internally, to learn. If you have an exceptionally able child, you'll be used to being woken up at unearthly hours by an excited 4-year-old wanting to tell you about something they've just found out from TV or in a book. Sometimes, their desire to communicate or physically manifest what's in their head outstrips their physical development, and this can lead to huge frustration for them.

When my son was a toddler, he 'gave up' drawing. We'd had weeks of him screwing up paper and throwing it across the room followed by this final meltdown, because he was trying to draw a car. In his head he knew exactly what this car looked like, but his young, uncoordinated hands couldn't produce the photograph-quality image in his head, which is what he was aiming for, and in the end he simply stopped trying.

A few months later, we were on a trip to London and I took him to the National Gallery, bypassing our usual favourites in favour of the abstract art section, particularly the works of Jackson Pollock. Learning how much people were willing to pay for these pieces got my son thinking and eventually he started drawing again.

7. They like to be in control

Terman's research into the lives of his 'Termites' found that intelligent people are often natural leaders, and that's certainly true – in fact, others will often look to them to assume a leadership or figurehead role even if they don't put themselves forward for one. Speaking from personal experience, however, there's more to this tendency than an innate willingness to command.

When your brain can rapidly think of all the possible outcomes for any given scenario, including the bad ones, anxiety can become a real issue – we'll explore this more later. Making sure your life is kept tightly under control helps make that anxiety more manageable and reduces unpredictability, so it's quite common for our bright sparks to want to know every last detail of what they're going to be involved with ahead of time, and resent misinformation or people who just want to 'wing it'.

8. They prefer adults (or solitude) to other children

Does this scene sound familiar? Your child has been invited to a birthday party. They don't particularly want to go, but you believe it'll do them good to work on their social skills, so an RSVP is duly sent. You can see their face fall as you arrive to a horde of over-excited youngsters racing here, there and everywhere, but you drop them off and spend the next couple of hours waiting anxiously before returning to collect them.

The rest of the kids are still tearing around happily. Yours, meanwhile, can be found sitting in the kitchen along with the adults, sharing a cup of tea and discussing the merits of a well-funded mass-transit system, home-grown tomatoes or how to go about terraforming Mars. If there's no adult-level conversation to be had, many bright kids will be far happier pursuing their own interests in isolation than they will be interacting with those who aren't as high-speed as they are.

9. They're quick learners

As a teacher, I was taught that the average child needs to read a word roughly 50 times before it sticks in their vocabulary, and requires two weeks of lessons and regular practice before they've understood and assimilated a new concept. Bright sparks, on the other hand, rarely need telling twice, and can use their amazing memories to recall facts from long ago. As one mother told me: "Walking home from school one time, my daughter told me that she thought she was the best at listening in class, because she understood what the teacher said first time – but the teacher had to explain the same thing again and again for the rest of the class, as they clearly don't listen."

10. They're aware of world events

As a gifted child, you can pick up on what's happening in the world around you and issues others are facing, even if you don't understand the context. Growing up, I was confounded as to why American soldiers were fighting gorillas (as opposed to guerrillas) in Vietnam. One mother told me that her 5-year-old daughter declared that she was going to stop buying dolls because, in her own words, "they contain too much plastic and it's not good for the planet. Maybe we could write to them and see if they can make them out of something recyclable."

Unfortunately, the emotional development needed to contextualise and deal with this knowledge often isn't there, just like when they absorb facts related to their hobbies and interests. My son would cry himself to sleep at night because he couldn't do anything to help children starving in Africa, and in the end I had to stop him from watching the news.

11. They love to talk...

Compulsive communication is a classic example of gifted behaviour. For one thing, it's so much quicker than writing or even typing can be. You only have to get a group of gifted people together and give them a subject they're excited about, then watch as the words-per-minute counter starts to rise until they're conversing at what for many people would be unintelligibly fast. Emphatic body language being used to underscore whatever point is being made is also a common sight, so it can be wise to keep a watchful eye on your drink.

12. ... and ask questions!

"Mummy, why don't sheep wipe their bottoms?" (Patricia, aged 4)

"How do trees eat carbon dioxide when they don't have a mouth?" (Henry, aged 3)

Awkward questions are a gifted child's speciality! Not that they mean to be awkward, of course, they just can't help thinking about these things – what would happen if the world stopped spinning, why can't other animals talk, how long it would take the house to be buried in fallen leaves, and so on. As a parent, you soon learn to be wary of any sentence that begins "What if...?"

 Looking back at the list above, how many of these traits do you recognise in those around you? How about in yourself?

These are by no means all of the common attributes that gifted children tend to share. With this many signals, you might think a bright spark would be simple to spot. Sometimes, however, these signs get misdiagnosed and the child in question is labelled not as gifted, but as ADHD or autistic instead.

Why would this be? Well, throughout my career I've noticed there are many 'similarities in presentation' – that is, shared traits that lead to similar patterns of behaviour – but actually, they have very different root causes and need to be managed differently.

To understand why this happens and how the two situations are very different, let's take a look at some unusual behaviours that, at least on the face of it, are shared by both children with high IQs and children who, while they may or may not also be bright, have been diagnosed with Autistic Spectrum Disorder (ASD). There are six main shared traits:

■ Being prone to anxiety

■ Experiencing social difficulties when interacting with others

■ Having special or unusual interests about which they're hugely knowledgeable

■ Suffering from emotional meltdown episodes

■ Crashing into a period of unresponsive behaviour

■ Extreme sensitivities to external stimulation.

We'll look more deeply at how and why these traits manifest in gifted children, as well as ways to cope with them, throughout this book. When we list some of the high-level causes, though, some key differences soon become apparent:

Symptoms	ASD	High IQ
Anxiety	Change of routine, such as exams or school trips	Overthinking or a fear of failure
Social Difficulties	Play is repetitive, object-based and lacking in imagination	Lack of people on their level. Play is sophisticated and complex
Special/Unusual Interests	Tend to be long-term and all-consuming	Will do a topic to death then move on to another
Meltdowns	Overload. Too much going on or out of their comfort zone	Frustration at being an 'old head' on young shoulders
Crashing	Overload or not understanding what is required of them	Overthinking, anxiety. Emotional understanding can't keep up
Sensitivities	Difficulty internalising information from senses, for example, hunger, pain	Lack of filtering; can take in lots of information quickly

Due to these similarities, it's both unprofessional and dangerous for anyone who isn't qualified to try to diagnose a child based purely on observations, let alone share it with the child's parents. Anyone with suspicions or concerns should always share them with a professional rather than leaping to conclusions.

Symptoms and Common Causes

What, then, of those who might have slipped through the net during childhood and went on to become gifted grown-ups? Can they also be spotted by a discerning eye? It's possible, but it can be a trickier prospect. Children and adults behave very differently regardless – well, most of the time – but one key difference is that most adults are much better at self-regulation and hiding unusual aspects of themselves. My son, when quizzed on the matter, admitted that he'd have to be extremely bored to repeat his festive supermarket performance nowadays.

Gifted children will be openly precocious, while adults generally learn to temper that part of their personality during day-to-day life – unless, that is, they're in a field where precociousness is either encouraged or not actively discouraged. We're expected to conform if we're working in an office or other shared space, while academics, scientists or those in creative disciplines may find they have more freedom to express their eccentricities.

As most people are not academics or scientists though, the expectations of adult life tend to temper many of the traits we've examined in this chapter. After many of my lectures, I've been approached by astonished people who tell me that I've just accurately painted a picture of their life. Having never been spotted as gifted in their youth, and having learned how to mask their differences as they've got older, these adults have never even suspected that they might be highly intelligent, let alone been in a position to make use of that intelligence. This is a real shame, for as we'll see in the next chapter, there are plenty of advantages afforded to those possessed of a uniquely buzzy brain.

Chapter 3

Advantages of
Being Gifted

Chapter 3:
Advantages of Being Gifted

Whether you're a bright youngster or well into your adult years, telling your peers that you're possessed of a high IQ can be a bit of a double-edged sword. Most of the time the reaction will be simple curiosity, but there will always be those whose response tends more toward resentment. They might believe that you're boasting, for one thing, especially if they assume that 'being clever' only leads to positive consequences and so you're flaunting an advantage over them.

On the whole, though, people tend to be both impressed and inquisitive when they find out you've got a high IQ, as long as it wasn't because you started flashing your Mensa membership card around. In fact, the precise figure of your IQ will probably be one of their first questions, along with whether or not it makes you smarter than Albert Einstein (or someone like him). Next, they're likely to ask what it's like to be bright.

Questions like this, about how it feels to be brainy, are perfectly well-intentioned – but they can also leave you flummoxed. After all, it's hard to answer how it feels to 'be' something when you've never 'been' anything, or anyone, else. You might never have stopped to consider the ways in which you work differently from other people, or what aspects of life they struggle with that seem to come naturally to you. So, what are the upsides to having a high IQ, and how does one take advantage of them?

As we discussed in the previous chapter, one positive aspect of a high intellect is being able to absorb and retain information far more swiftly and easily than others. While this can sometimes be frustrating when you're trying to work along to a set curriculum and everything seems to be unfurling incredibly slowly, it's hugely beneficial when it comes to learning new skills in a hurry. Learning your way around an unfamiliar piece of software at a new job, getting to grips with the rules of a sport or deftly recalling the names of people you bump into at a party (as well as the names of their kids and pets) can all help you hit the ground running while other people are still tying their metaphorical shoelaces.

Often, these tendencies will get picked up on by those around you, whether you're at school or at work. Even if you're new, and regardless of whether or not you put yourself forward for positions of responsibility, it's common for people to start seeking your opinions anyway. You may even find queues of people forming at your desk wanting to ask you this or that, assuming that whatever their question is you'll either know the answer or know how to find out. You'll almost certainly get recruited for the office pub quiz team if there is one!

Being a quick study can open up a lot of choices in your adult life, but choices are all they are. Intelligence does not mean you're destined to go and become a neuroscientist, high-profile lawyer or business mogul. Nor are you somehow squandering your giftedness if you don't decide to pursue that sort of lifestyle! There are plenty of bright people who will choose to eschew an all-consuming career in favour of a 9-to-5 job that allows them to focus their intellect elsewhere. Intelligence presents you with more options for yourself and your prospects, but it certainly doesn't – and shouldn't – pigeonhole you into jobs you don't enjoy. If anything, it can help you avoid them.

Outside of the workplace, your innate capacity for problem-solving will manifest itself in all kinds of useful ways. You'll encounter situations where something goes wrong and, while other people are standing around looking stumped, you'll already be googling the solution or dreaming up one of your own. As we've been discussing IQ tests so far, it's easy to presume that the term 'problem-solving' only means grasping abstract concepts and spotting patterns, but in fact intelligence also helps you deal with everyday obstacles like planning a trip at short notice, staying cool in a heatwave or fitting a large pile of groceries into the boot of your car.

When my son was young, we went on a day trip to London. I had some Mensa meetings to attend in the day and then, for the evening, we'd managed to get tickets to one of the first wrestling events that the WWE (Or the World Wrestling Federation, as it was named back then) ever held in the UK. Unfortunately, having taken them off to read during the journey, my son managed to break his glasses in half shortly before we arrived.

Without an intact pair of specs, there was no way he'd be able to make out anything that was happening 10 feet away, let alone watch what was happening in a distant wrestling ring.

While I went to my appointments, my son and his Dad spent what should have been a pleasant day's sightseeing trekking around London, searching for a way to repair a broken pair of glasses. Local opticians were sympathetic but unable to help repair the frames at short notice, and it took a long time to hunt down a shop that sold an adhesive glue suitable for sealing the two halves back together. After a lot of false starts and frustration, the glasses were repaired by the time we were reunited for dinner before heading to the wrestling.

Around 10 minutes before the show was due to start, after we'd all taken our seats, fate struck a second time. The glue gave way and the glasses fell apart once again. Needless to say, we were all more than a little disconsolate. It was at that point we realised that we were sitting a few rows in front of a St. John Ambulance crew, who were on hand in case anyone was to be injured or taken ill. We decided to approach them with the stricken spectacles, reasoning that the worst they would do is shrug helplessly and send us back to our seats.

Much to our delight, the crew were able to make liberal use of sticking plasters and other materials to patch up the glasses so my son could see the show. (The day's events had so exhausted him that he fell asleep a few minutes later, but that's another story.) This tale remains one of my favourite examples of how a high IQ affords you the ability to think outside the box, spotting possible connections and linking together seemingly disconnected elements – in this case, a pair of broken specs and spotting someone who would have access to a first-aid kit – to find a solution where others cannot.

Take a look at the following thought experiment and consider what your response would be if you were in that situation:

As part of a contest to win a million pounds, you've been dropped off in the middle of an unfamiliar city with no belongings apart from a credit card you can use for funds. Your job is to find and purchase a 'Humdinger'. Sounds simple, except you've got no idea what a 'Humdinger' is nor where to find one. To make matters even more complicated, you can't understand the language of anyone you meet. How do you go about buying a Humdinger?

What solution(s) did you come up with? We put the same question to a number of bright adults and children, and their responses help show the sheer variety of solutions intelligence helps you conjure up when faced with obstacles. We've included a few replies at the end of the chapter.

Able as they are to take in and process lots of information at once, it's possible for many intelligent people to swiftly pick up on social cues and react accordingly. This is easier for adults since, as we've mentioned, they've generally learned to moderate their own impulses in order not to stand out from the crowd. These 'social chameleons' can go one stage further and read a room when they enter it, quickly assessing the people they'll be interacting with before modifying their own behaviour to help ingratiate themselves.

These behavioural modifications can involve anything from altering body language and posture, picking particular topics of conversation while avoiding others, changing to a different vocabulary or even adjusting their accent. This isn't done to deceive anyone, and with enough practice it often happens subconsciously as a way of making other people feel comfortable around them. If two social circles happen to collide, it can make the social chameleon feel extremely anxious as they try to juggle 'being' two individuals at once.

Chapter 3: Advantages of Being Gifted

Luckily for the chameleons, being able to think on your feet comes with the territory. When placed in the spotlight or under pressure, gifted sorts excel at coming up with excuses and deferrals that are far more creative and convincing than 'the dog ate my homework'. It's the same kind of mental agility that makes for swift repartee and rapid-fire comebacks when being heckled or challenged, and is likely one of the reasons so many successful stand-up comedians are bright people – there's much more to the job than simply reciting a list of memorised jokes out on stage.

Multi-tasking is another advantage to having a large working memory. Being able to bounce backwards and forwards between different activities, remember the thrust of several concurrent conversations or read and enjoy different articles at once are all very useful skills. The downside, however, is that when bright sparks do need to focus all of their attention on one particular task it can be very difficult for them to do so.

A bluebottle buzzing against the window, song lyrics or a voice on the radio, the temptation to peek at social media… All of these can become significant distractions for a bright brain, even if other people wouldn't notice them. Sometimes, intelligent people need to cut themselves off from all external stimulation in order to concentrate completely on the matter at hand. Woe betide anyone who dares break the concentration of a bright spark when they've finally got themselves into the zone!

While there are undoubtedly many and varied advantages to being highly intelligent, it's crucial that parents and children alike understand that being bright is no guarantee of success. Likewise, it should go without saying that a high IQ is absolutely no reason to feel superior or believe yourself to be inherently 'better' than those around you. An active brain is no excuse for a swelled head! Bright people are just as capable as anyone else of making bad decisions, missing the obvious solutions, forgetting why they've walked into a room, missing birthdays and other appointments, burning the dinner, tripping over the cat, losing their car keys or hurting someone's feelings. Sometimes all in the same day.

Nor is there any guarantee that intelligent people will be inherently more kind, selfless, motivated, loving or considerate than their neighbours. In short, nothing about intelligence makes you a good person, or even a nice person. Whatever your intellect, there are many other factors that will decide what kind of human being you are. If you're lucky, most of them will be under your control. At best, you'll be able to leverage your intelligence to become a well-rounded, successful and compassionate individual. It's not always going to be plain sailing, though. As we shall see in the following chapters, gifted people also face unique challenges of their own.

Sample answers to Humdinger activities on page 35

You buy the first snow dome you see wherever you go and I bet it'll be a humdinger! (Tina)

Okay, I buy a Phone so I have Internet, Google the language and download a translate program, Google regional dialects, and then Google Humdingers, see what it throws up, decide on what I think the most likely candidate is, then where to buy it, or order online to an Amazon drop box. (John)

Buy a laptop and find a cafe with wi-fi. Create some pictures of T-shirts with whatever graphics package the laptop has on it, "Official Humdinger Merch" blazoned across them. Register the domain official-humdinger-merch.com, throw an e-commerce store together on Squarespace and start taking orders. If you receive a cease-and-desist from Humdinger Corp., you'll have a paper-trail to follow to their legal department. Give them a call and ask to be put through to sales. If they never get in contact, at least you might now have a decent source of income from your new online store to make you feel better about not winning the £1m. (Edward)

Buy a phone, change the language to English and ask Siri! (Darragh, age 6.)

Chapter 4

Physical Challenges

Chapter 4:
Physical Challenges

Let's be honest – no parent wants to hear that their child is likely to face a number of unusual obstacles as they grow and mature, least of all when those obstacles arise through no fault of their own. That's why, before we look more deeply at the unique hurdles faced by gifted youngsters, it's crucial to stress that the next couple of chapters will not be a litany of woe. There's a good reason why the cover of this book is not a sign reading 'Abandon Hope, All Who Enter Here'!

As we examine each of the possible trials that lie ahead, I'll be discussing ways to spot signs of trouble ahead of time, as well as offering practical solutions for when problems do arise. That said, it's important to remember that the perfect instruction manual for children doesn't exist; everyone's situation is different. Even so, the aim of the next few chapters is to help parents, teachers and psychologists spot some of the common warning signs and know what to do about them. As we go, let's consider one particular child as an example: Ella.

Ella is 7 years old, and she loves to learn and read. When left to her own devices she tells stories to her toys and puts on performances for them. Physically, Ella is quite unassuming, within the average height and weight ranges for a child of her age. Her IQ, however, falls within the top 2% for 7-year-olds, giving her a mental age of 12. More specifically she has a reading age of 12, a comprehension age of 10 and a maths age of 8 years, 6 months. (These differences in performance are quite normal for a gifted child as reading comprehension and maths skills are also affected by education and experience.)

If we were to examine Ella's motor-coordination, we would find that despite her intelligence, she's still struggling to ride a tricycle and needs her parents to help tie her shoelaces. At school, she sometimes needs assistance getting dressed after PE lessons – in other words, physically, she is a year or two behind what would be expected for a girl of 7. She struggles to find friends at school and spends most playtimes either singing to herself or reading one of her favourite books. In terms of social development, as we'll see later, Ella is also a year or so behind her actual age.

Last week, Ella's Dad had to go up to her room and give her a hug after hearing her crying. She'd read about a war between two countries in a magazine, and had learned that some people had died, others had lost their homes and nobody had enough food or clean water. She desperately wanted to help them and thought that sending her dinner might work. The enormity of the problem, and her inability to solve it, had made her feel hopeless and upset. Instead, she decided to ask Father Christmas for a van filled with food so that she and her family could drive to the country and deliver it to those in need.

In Ella, we have a little girl whose ability levels range from 5 to 12 years old, all wrapped up in one single child, and that's not easy for anyone. Her emotional development and life experience may be age appropriate, but she can understand more than they allow her to cope with. We'll be returning to Ella throughout the next couple of chapters, but you may already recognise a few of her behaviours in your own offspring.

As is evident in Ella's case, gifted children display asynchronous development – that is to say, as they grow, their physical and mental capabilities do not progress at an even rate. By definition, a bright child's intellectual development is ahead of where you'd expect, but just because a 9-year-old can think at a 12-year-old level, it obviously doesn't mean they also possess the body of a 12-year-old – therefore, there's a developmental disparity.

Learning Skills

Even when a gifted child's physical development is age appropriate and there are no other difficulties or disabilities, they're still an 'old head' on a young body. They will understand life's protocols and how to behave, but will be held back from doing so by their age, their size or their motor skills – just like my son when he 'gave up' on art.

Trying to dress themselves for school like the older children do only to fail and be called 'cute', struggling to create a complicated LEGO masterpiece, attempting to clean out the guinea pig cage by themselves or learning to perform a magic trick that delighted them on TV… these are all things that will cause our bright sparks huge frustration, particularly when they don't comprehend the reasons for their failure. While it's impossible to alleviate these frustrations entirely, I've used a number of techniques, as both a mother and teacher, that can help allay them.

At home, allow the child to do as much as they're able to help. Even young children are able to fetch things, take used towels to the laundry basket, lay the table for dinner or strip the sheets off a bed. Yes, you could do those things faster and more efficiently. You might even need to redo the job entirely after they've finished and aren't watching, but if afterwards you tell them "You're such a help now that you're (their age), you couldn't do that when you were only (a younger age)" then you'll give them a sense of progression and an understanding that physical limitations don't last forever.

Conversely, beginning a sentence with "I think you're old enough to…" shows that when the time is right, you will let them do things, and makes it easier for them to swallow a bitter pill when you forbid them to do something for safety reasons. Whenever I hosted family get-togethers, my son, nephew and niece were all given jobs to help me. I'd ask them to arrange packets of crisps nicely in a basket, or to carry a tray of cakes to the table (while I shadowed behind just in case). Hot things and sharp things were not to be touched – those jobs could wait until they were older – but we never had any accidents, nor were any rules broken.

More formally, I teach basic child development to 5 to 7-year-olds as part of my gifted child workshops. To begin with, we look at videos of newborn babies and talk about how the children in the group were once like that – unable to do anything for themselves. The children find it hilarious to see footage of babies learning to feed themselves or to walk, tasks that they of course are now perfectly comfortable with. They're always keen to tell me of all the things they can do that babies can't.

Next, I ask them what would have happened if they, having fallen over as infants, had decided that walking was too hard and given up. More laughter follows as we imagine the consequences of having abandoned basic skills as a baby. The next logical step is to talk about how there are things that they still can't do because of their age, but explain that they'll be able to do them as they get older as long as they keep trying. (This is a good time to introduce them to the word 'resilience'.)

"I can't draw!" one 6-year-old declared during one of these workshops. I gave the child a sheet of paper and asked them to produce a line, then a circle, and so on. "There," I replied, "You can draw!"

The child stared at me scathingly. "Have you seen the work of Leonardo da Vinci?" he asked. At this point, another child piped up. "You will get better at drawing as you get older, but only if you practise!" My work was done!

Why does the physical development of more able children tend to lag behind their classmates? The answer is two-fold: firstly, when you're busy thinking, reading, wondering about black holes or composing music in your head, why waste any of your attention on a mundane task like dressing yourself when there are willing grown-ups around to help you? Secondly, and perhaps more importantly, if you get lots of enjoyment and positive feedback from the things you excel at, why would you want to spend time on tasks where you know you'll struggle or possibly fail entirely?

List the chores you avoid doing as an adult because you don't enjoy them or aren't very good at them. (Washing the car is one of mine.)

Getting to Sleep

One of the big physical challenges for gifted people, children and adults alike, is sleeping. Generally, you'll find that unless ADHD, illness or night terrors are a factor, bright children will be out like a light once they do fall asleep – but getting them there is another thing entirely.

Even as a tiny baby, my son fought against sleeping. He'd wriggle, yell and wave his arms around as, although he was exhausted, he wouldn't or couldn't, do the one thing that's vital to nodding off: relax. As an infant, the technique that worked for him was swaddling. I'd wrap him firmly (but not too tightly) in something light so he didn't get overheated, then hold him. He would shout, but after 30 seconds or so he'd be in a deep sleep, and after a minute or two I could place him back in his cradle and loosen the swaddling so that he could move freely when he woke up.

I knew to try this trick because it worked on me when I was young, and it's one I learned from a family friend who used to babysit me. As an adult, I find that even in the hottest weather I still need my feet covered if I'm to sleep in bed. Of course, swaddling only works for so long – your teenage son or daughter may object to you pouncing on them and wrapping them in a sheet – but some parents I know make use of weighted blankets, the kind normally used for autistic children. Sleeping bags also work well.

What doesn't seem to work well for bright minds are the traditional bedtime rituals that one might use for other children, like baths or bedtime stories. Years of experience and experimentation have taught me that a single-focus activity works best for our bright sparks. Thus, at bedtime, keep talking to a minimum. This is no time to be discussing the events of the day, upcoming exams, tonight's *Danger Mouse* or any other worries. Instead, the would-be sleeper should engage with something that takes all of their focus and allows no time for their mind to drift. Reading silently doesn't work – how many times have you scanned a page from top to bottom while working through a book, only to find you haven't taken in a word of it because your mind was elsewhere? Reading aloud requires focus and is more effective.

Other activities that I've seen work in the past are Sudoku, audiobooks and certain video games. I've just heard a gasp of horror at the thought of giving a child video games at bedtime, but it works! Of course, I'm not talking about multiplayer games like *Fortnite* or any mobile apps that play adverts every 30 seconds. I'm talking about games like *Tetris* or *Bejeweled*; games where looking away from the screen for a moment or allowing your mind to wander will cause you to lose.

To this day, I use a combination of these activities to draw my focus and help me relax before bed. This normally results in my climbing under the covers because I'm physically tired, and half an hour later my husband will come up, take the Sudoku book or tablet out of my hands while I sleep, and turn the lights out.

One other thing you can try that works surprisingly well is the simple act of balancing on one leg, because it requires discipline and concentration. As a bonus, you can do it right by the side of your bed. It's also an excellent exercise for children as it has the secondary benefit of improving balance and coordination and, as something they'll get better at as they practise, is another way to convey the notion of resilience.

Difficulties and Disabilities

Being exceptionally able does not preclude you from having to deal with physical, health or other difficulties. Gifted children are as likely as any other to live with asthma, allergies, autism, ADHD, or cerebral palsy as any other member of the population. Suffice it to say, practical advice on dealing with all of those conditions goes far beyond the scope of this book.

Equally, though, it's possible to prosper even when suffering from severe physical conditions. One young man I used to teach came from a very difficult social background, was confined to a wheelchair because of his cerebral palsy and, as it transpired, was incredibly bright. Despite his difficulties, his attendance at school was excellent and his work ethic was second to none. Not only did he achieve academically but he went on to join the school council, a wheelchair basketball team and accomplished many other things. Another went on to become Head Boy, despite living with ASD and spending most of his first school year curled up under a table. No matter our IQ, it's not our difficulties that define us, but how we face them that makes us who we are.

Chapter 5

Emotional Challenges

Chapter 5:
Emotional Challenges

Let's return to Ella. In the previous chapter I mentioned that she'd been lying awake, and upset, thinking about children in a distant part of the world who didn't have enough food to eat. It's a common misconception among parents and adults in general that if a child is old enough to understand a concept intellectually, they must also be equipped with the mental toolkit to deal with the concept on an emotional level. Nothing could be further from the truth – as with physical development, our emotional development tends to be age-appropriate regardless of how bright we are.

In this chapter, we'll look at surmounting some of the challenges that can arise from a gulf between intellect and emotional maturity, but first let's examine why emotional development is more than just a matter of thinking your way through a disturbing situation until you make your peace with it. Even as adults, we still find ourselves affected by news of tragedy and suffering – understanding the root causes of seismic activity doesn't diminish our sympathy for anyone who lost their home to an earthquake, for example.

A key part of our emotional development is life experience and, for obvious reasons, we almost always accrue that at an age-appropriate rate. We're not born knowing what a fire is, let alone that we shouldn't stick our fingers into the flames. If the adults around us aren't being watchful and we do end up touching the fire, that particular life experience will not only be physically painful but possibly even emotionally traumatic, and may go on to affect us for the rest of our lives. Sooner or later, as we get older, we're bound to end up accidentally touching something hot, but hopefully not until we've learned enough to know that the pain will be temporary and how to avoid repeating the mistake.

Our emotional development begins with our parents or other major caregivers. Once our most basic needs – food as required, affectionate touch, swift responses when we need something, and so on – have been met, then our interaction with other humans becomes of paramount importance and determines how we'll go on to cope with the world.

The first stage is proximity, where being held, hugged and touched keeps us feeling safe and secure. Joint attention with our caregiver, as we place our faces side by side or focus on the same things, helps us understand that not only are we not alone but are experiencing the wonders of the world in a similar way to others. Later, sharing develops our rudimentary interaction skills. Next time a baby offers you some of their mushed-up banana, think twice before refusing! You'll see the obvious joy on their face even if you only pretend to eat some.

Activity

Your baby is learning to walk but, as is normal, is falling down a lot at first. When they fall and begin to cry, how do you react?

A) Ignore them. They do it all the time and it's part of learning to walk.

B) Complete a quick visual check to ensure they're not hurt and encourage them to try again.

C) Go "Oh dear," give them a hug and take them to do something else.

D) Run over, check them from top-to-toe and give them a big hug.

E) Complete a quick visual check to ensure they're not hurt, then give them a cheer and a big round of applause.

Solution: Well, every choice will work to an extent, but they each have a number of potential impacts (both positive and negative) upon the baby's emotional development. Let's consider:

A) You may just be teaching the child the lesson that no one will come for you when you cry, making them less trusting of you and others in the future.

B) Works nicely. The child knows you're there if needed but also that this isn't one of those times – there's no need to make a mountain out of a molehill.

C) Works nicely, however, we've seen that children – particularly gifted children – tend to give up on things they find difficult. Are you perhaps teaching that this is a good approach?

D) Only do this if it's warranted. An overreaction can lead to an anxious baby who cries if they're the least bit doubtful of the situation they're in.

E) I watched my friend's family do this. The crying stopped, then the baby started clapping and smiling too. He even 'fell over' on purpose a few more times to ensure everyone was clapping – the 'failure' had become a success as he now had a new way to interact with the world around him. I went on to use this same approach with my own son.

Chapter 5: Emotional Challenges

Once the relationship between the child and the caregiver has been established, we encourage them to develop self-regulation, as in the example above. As you can see, even an innocuous act can have an impact on how the child behaves later in life. At the same time, children will model their self-regulation on how they see their caregiver tackling life events. Parents will sometimes tell me "My child is very shy, but then I was a shy child too." More often than not, further investigation tells me that the parent is still shy and prefers to avoid large social gatherings and interactions with strangers. As a natural consequence, their child – who instinctively trusts the parent's judgement calls – does too.

As part of this developmental process, one of the things we teach our children is emotional control. That's not something they're born with; it comes from watching their caregivers respond to life events, and so the ability to process and internalise emotions comes as the child spends time with the caregiver, matures and gets life experience of their own.

Clearly, Ella's family have modelled empathy and caring for those in need as she's been growing up, so that's part of her emotional repertoire – she feels and cares for those who have been caught up in the war she read about. At 7 years old, however, she still believes in magic and Santa Claus. Her life experience is limited to her family, friends and classmates, and situations she encounters at home, school or occasionally on holiday. She's never experienced real hunger, homelessness or trauma. Therefore, when she learns about these concepts, she has no way of reconciling them with her own life experiences and internalising the emotions they cause in her. They swirl around in her head, making her anxious and giving her bad dreams.

For our brightest children, this kind of emotional 'clogged drain' won't be limited to one event at a time, and over a longer period of time several sets of concerns are likely to be causing them anxiety. These ideas can come from anywhere: books the child has been reading, hearing adults or older children talking inappropriately, movies and TV or even things they've learned at school. Much as we may wish to completely shield our children from knowledge that's going to cause them stress in this way, even if it were possible to do so, it can be argued that we shouldn't. Just as when they deal with physical challenges, it's important that we help our children learn to face life's misfortunes and develop emotional resilience, providing a strong adult presence to talk through any worries and help provide some perspective. Let's look at some ways parents and caregivers can take the reins and teach some coping strategies.

Don't Over-inform

When dealing with big, heavy or important topics, I will always advise parents to disclose only the minimum amount of information necessary to allay the child's fears. The more detail you give, the more likely it is that you'll raise further questions and worries in their mind.

When my son was 4, he called me into his room and informed me that he would never be able to get married. The reason for this upcoming life of solitude, he explained, was that he knew married people had families, but he didn't know how to make a baby. At that point, I could have launched into the 'birds and bees' talk, but at 4 I felt he was simply too young for that kind of explanation.

Instead, I asked him if he was planning to get married in the next couple of months and hadn't told me. He laughed, breaking the tension he obviously felt at having to confront the subject, and I told him that if he still didn't know by the time he'd organised the wedding, I'd fill him in on what he needed to know. This did the trick – the worry was taken away because the actual details of the answer weren't his concern, but now he knew that an answer existed and that it was in the hands of a trusted adult.

Anchor the Problem to a Solved Experience

In Ella's case, a two-pronged approach can be effective. The first step is to anchor the problem by equating the event to a similar, less severe event in the child's life that was ultimately solved, and then secondly to assure them that solutions also exist for the larger problem. This will help Ella process the emotions she's feeling using her own life experience.

In Ella's case, her parents could say something like "Ella, do you remember that time we went on a picnic, and all of our food fell in the water so we couldn't eat it? We were so hungry by the time we got home but we found a fish and chip shop that was still open. I think those children in your book are even hungrier than that, but there are agencies run by adults who go out and take food to help hungry children." Ella now not only has an emotional grounding that allows her to empathise with what the children are feeling, but the knowledge that people are working to deal with the problem and she's not the only one who's worried.

Provide a Sense of Control

The individuals in the world who are in a position to do anything about global issues like climate change or famine are few and far between, and your gifted child isn't one of them – at least, not yet. That doesn't mean, though, that there aren't safe, simple actions that our bright sparks can take to help them feel like they're back in control of the problem, once you've explained how what they're doing will help.

Sometimes the influences can be external. In May 1988, Sport Aid, the second sport-themed campaign of its type, was held across the UK to the accompaniment of a charity single put out by Status Quo. Despite having no interest in sport, my son had learned about the famine in Africa and decided he wanted to help them. I accompanied him from door to door as he took his sponsor sheet around to our neighbours, and later watched (with his asthma inhalers close at hand) as he donned an oversized 'Run the World' T-shirt and spent his Saturday doing laps around the area. Several of the neighbours came out to cheer him on, possibly because it was one of

the first times they'd seen him running around outside. Being able to do something, no matter how small, helped him find the emotional grounding point to work through the anxiety.

Detect and Distract

The busy brains of bright people think and analyse everything non-stop. Sometimes there doesn't need to be a particular trigger to send our minds down a rabbit hole of concerns and worries. Something as simple as "the boss wants to see me tomorrow and I don't know why" can cause us to spiral as we map out every possible scenario in our heads. Even when we're grown, we can find it tough to reconcile a situation against our life experience when we have no concrete information. Instead, we overthink our way to any number of eventualities ranging from disastrous (we're being fired), to desirable (we're being made CEO), to downright daft (they're sending us to the Arctic Circle to start a new branch).

As adults, the trick is to catch ourselves in the act. Once we realise we're spiralling, we can take a moment to right ourselves using a single-focus activity of the kind discussed in the previous chapter until our anxiety is diminished, then turn our attentions to other techniques to get on top of our thoughts. Children have less of an ability for self-assessment, so as parents or caregivers, we can learn to recognise the signs in them and give them activities that we know will slowly ease them out of the emotional whirlpool we call overthinking.

White Lies

As we've already discussed, tempting as it might be to protect our children from the scarier aspects of the world, they won't develop resilience if we do. I'm not going to advocate telling children that famine is overstated or that climate change isn't a problem even if the truth is upsetting to them. That said, earlier in this chapter I mentioned that Ella is of an age where she still believes in Santa Claus. A very common 'white lie' of that kind can sometimes be helpful.

Chapter 5: Emotional Challenges

Now, obviously, not every family teaches their children that there's going to be a visit from a magical, red-suited man who'll pop down the chimney overnight to deliver gifts. Not only do different cultures have different traditions, but some parents simply choose not to engage their children with that particular fiction. Even so, I'd hope that those who don't participate can appreciate that those parents who do play along and put out mince pies on Christmas Eve aren't doing so to cruelly deceive their offspring, but to help make a cold, hectic time of year seem that bit more positive and magical – not to mention encouraging youngsters to remain well behaved while they're out of their regular routine.

While not everyone may feel comfortable telling white lies to their children, even with the best of intentions, I'd like to close the chapter out by sharing a technique I dreamed up that worked wonders when my son was having a phase of night terrors. He'd wake up calling for me, and a hug and a drink of water would only provide a temporary break before he sank back into the same nightmares.

One night, I'd just finished watching an episode of *Star Trek* when he called for me. Going upstairs, I told my son that I'd learned a new way to remove bad dreams entirely. I ritualised the procedure as I was going along – "lie back, slow your breathing and look at me" – and then placed my hand on his face in a passable imitation of the Vulcan Mind Meld, staring deeply into his eyes before informing him that I had withdrawn all of the bad dreams from his head. This worked like a charm, and he spent the rest of the night asleep without a murmur.

If he was feeling anxious, my son soon got into the habit of calling for me before bed to come and take the bad dreams away. As he got older, he needed this ritual less and less, and by the time he was old enough to discover *Star Trek* for himself and recognise the gesture I'd borrowed from Mr. Spock, he was also old enough to understand why I had created the fiction and why it had worked for logical, if entirely human, reasons.

Chapter 6

Social Challenges

Chapter 6:
Social Challenges

When do parents start to suspect that their offspring might be bright? It's a question I'm often asked and, speaking personally, I find that many times I'm contacted by parents shortly after their son or daughter has started nursery or playgroup, especially if it's their first child. Up until that point the child has spent most of his or her time as a perfectly normal member of the family, and it's only when they begin to mix with other children that alarm bells start to ring.

As other parents start to pass comments like "they're very forward, aren't they?" or ask you how your child knows so much, you might start to spot that the other children in the group aren't doing the things yours does naturally – things that seemed totally natural when you had no point of reference. Let's take a closer look at the kinds of social challenges that await our bright sparks.

Heightened Empathy

When they first arrive at the Mother and Toddler group, children are generally at the stage of development where they're beginning to explore the environment and play with toys, but this generally happens in isolation or along with the caregiver. Cooperative play won't start for another couple of years yet and, to toddlers, other children are pretty much just part of the scenery. The mental universe they inhabit, their 'awareness bubble', is practically skintight. Toys are discarded on the floor the minute they're no longer interesting, at which point they might as well stop existing.

We'll talk more about awareness bubbles later on, but as an example, consider this familiar scene: a toddler in a doctor's waiting room, a shoe shop or at a friend's birthday party gets totally fixated on something and wanders away, engrossed. A moment later, they realise they don't know where they are. Immediately, they shout out and begin to cry until the caregiver 'rescues' them, and stay close at heel for a while after that.

Emotional self-regulation is non-existent – at that age, we still rely on others to moderate our feelings and behaviour.

Not so our bright sparks. These are the children who will wander around the room, picking up the toys and putting them back in their places. These are the children who not only notice when another child falls, but go to give them help. They're also the children who will get anxious and cry if other children are crying or being told off. The oblivious behaviour of other youngsters isn't just baffling to a gifted child, it can actually be upsetting. When you're at home or with a parent, you at least have a reliable adult voice to check in with if you're feeling confused. At nursery, that voice sometimes disappears.

No Chance to Practise

My son had been to playgroup a grand total of three times. After his third session, he came home and informed me that he no longer needed to attend because, he said, he'd read all of the books and most of the toys were ones he had at home. I explained that the point of going to playgroup was to make friends and mix with the other children there.

Hands went onto young hips in his classic 'don't you know anything' pose. "Mummy," he replied. "They don't know their colours. They can't speak in sentences. What am I supposed to talk to them about?"

On the surface, this is an anecdote about a little boy who has nothing in common with his peers and finds himself isolated, which would be bad enough, but there's also a deeper problem at work. The obvious gulf meant that for the next two years, my son would have no opportunity to practise his own social skills, except with patient adults. As a result, his own development would inevitably end up falling behind where it should have been – after all, there's a lot more to socialising than the topic of conversation. I did insist that he kept on going to playgroup as, even if it was hardly an ideal situation, at least he'd be sharing a space with other children. Fortunately, a couple of weeks later, a little girl joined who was also a bright spark and the two quickly became inseparable. Playgroup was once again somewhere where my son wanted to be. I feel for those children who aren't lucky enough to find a kindred spirit.

The Wrong Kinds of Praise

When you are a gifted child, the sad truth is that adults, even well-meaning ones, will respond to you very differently without realising they're doing so. When you're young, this can have a profound effect on your social development, the knock-on effects of which don't become apparent until later life.

Let's consider Ella, our 7-year-old. When Ella was at nursery, she ran into many of the problems that gifted children face – even before she started to take in any form of formal education, she already knew her colours and loved to count how many buttons were in her Mum's sewing box. She could sing 'The Wheels on the Bus' perfectly every time. Needless to say, when Ella got to nursery and found that the day was structured around learning those same colours and numbers, she would soon get bored and wander off to read to the Peppa Pig doll.

What happens as a result of this scenario? The children who stayed in line get praised and get given a sticker for saying their colours right that day. Ella, however, doesn't get praise for already knowing them. Likewise, as the other children learn to share, to tidy away and sit nicely on their chair, these new behaviours will be praised by the nursery staff. They'll often forget to praise Ella for showing the same traits because, in her, these aren't new behaviours.

What the staff will do is quiz Ella on what she knows and respond positively to her intellect. The same is true when she goes to the shops or the hairdressers with her Mum and is told "Oh, here's our little genius! You can have a lolly if you tell me what seven plus three is." It's important to note that none of these people are doing this to be unkind to Ella, and it's all meant as positive reinforcement.

What Ella is learning, though, is that people like her not necessarily for who she is as a person, but because of what she knows and what she can do. At an age where she is still developing a sense of identity, most of her positive reinforcement is coming from being clever and using her intellect to perform. That can be a dangerous developmental path, and we'll see why later in the book.

Unless they're very lucky, by the time our gifted children start school they're already lagging behind in terms of their social experience and interaction. They have a lop-sided image of themselves, and little in common with their peers. They also have a sophisticated understanding of social rules and interests in common with much older children – except, of course, the older children don't want to play with them because they're so much younger.

It was at about this age that I had 'The Talk' with my son. He was a huge fan of the cartoon series *He-Man* and would race around the house waving his plastic sword and shouting "I have the power!" at an imaginary Skeletor. Of course, he wasn't the only one his age who liked *He-Man* and it was a popular choice of pretend play during breaks and lunchtimes at his primary school. That's why I was so concerned when I saw him walking right past the children playing his favourite game and sitting on a bench with a book instead.

When he got home, I asked him why he hadn't been playing *He-Man* with the others. He explained that he had tried a few times but had ultimately given up. "They're so silly," he explained. "They don't know that when you're dead, you can't just get up and run around anyway!" Clearly, his need for perfectionism and realism in his play was his main concern, not that his classmates needed an excuse for a proper run around.

I explained that he was going to have to be a little more tolerant of other people before giving up on them because, ultimately, we were the ones who were different and it needed to be us that made the effort to fit in. His interpersonal skill training started there.

Few of us are wealthy enough to buy a private island and populate it solely with people we like. As we share the same planet and breathe the same air, we have to learn to interact and get along with people from all walks of life. This can sometimes be tricky, as our first instinct is to form social bonds with people who operate at the same speed we do.

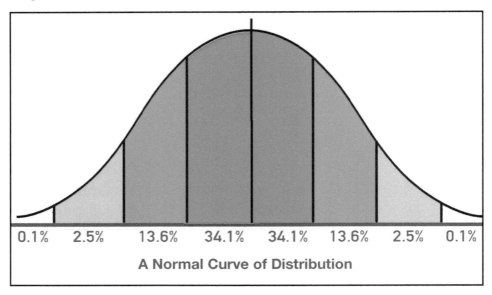

| 0.1% | 2.5% | 13.6% | 34.1% | 34.1% | 13.6% | 2.5% | 0.1% |

A Normal Curve of Distribution

The image above is a 'normal curve of distribution', also known as a bell curve, and it depicts a common pattern in nature. If I were to venture into the countryside (antihistamines in hand) and pick 100 daffodils at random to measure their height, I would find that while I would have some very tall daffodils and some very short ones, most of my crop would fall within a common size range. The same would be true of marrows, potatoes, turnips or anything else I was scrumping.

People's attributes also adhere to bell curves – their height, their weight and so on. This fact is used by governments, architects, clothing designers, engineers and more to design a world that is comfortable for the vast majority of us, even if the very tall or very short end up left out. The bell curve applies to intelligence, too. People who possess average or near-average intelligence make up the vast bulk of the population compared to people with exceptionally high or low intelligence.

If your IQ is around average and you fall in the centre of the bell curve, you will be surrounded by people like yourself. Whether it's at work, school or social situations, you'll have no trouble finding people to get on with who function at the same level you do. The further towards either end of the bell curve you go, the fewer people like you there are.

I should add that this problem socialising isn't the same as not having interests in common. As we've already discussed, bright people come from all walks of life and it's not true that all the people at the heart of the bell curve will only be talking about football while those at the far end are chatting about quantum computing. It doesn't help that people tend to assume you'll be working on a different level to them based on who you are, how you speak or what your job is.

When I first became a teacher, I was amazed at the number of people who, once they learned what my job was, would confess that they were a poor speller or terrible at maths. As if that's how I was judging everyone I met! Working in the games industry, my son encountered the same phenomenon. People would trip over themselves to tell him how computer illiterate they were, as if they feared there was going to be some impassable communication barrier unless they could talk to him in binary.

As a gifted child planted firmly at one end of the bell curve, then, not only do you have a smaller social group to choose from, you also need to find someone who shares your interests. These could be video games and sport, but equally might be esoteric topics like space travel or history – not an easy task when you're 6 years old! Later in life, the same hurdles can make it difficult to find professional and even life partners.

When I ran summer schools for young Mensans, I taught the attendees that aged from 4 to 8 years old. Each year was the same story: parents would arrive with their child clinging to their leg and tell me how young Freddy didn't like to make friends and was usually on his own in the playground. Their faces were a picture when they returned at the end of the day to find Freddy laughing, screaming and tearing around with the others. Looking at the group you'd have thought they were like any other children, although closer inspection would have shown a huge complexity in the subject matter, rules and interactions of their play. (If you're dead, you can't run around…)

At my workshops it becomes clear when watching exceptionally able children intermingling, particularly ones that haven't had much opportunity to socialise, that their social skill development is quite badly delayed. As a result, I tend to start with organised activities rather than free play and have to actively guide the children on how to interact with each other. Fortunately, we've seen that bright kids pick things up unusually quickly. Unless the children have additional difficulties, once they have made a few like-minded friends, they soon catch up with where you'd expect their social development to be.

Chapter 7

Sensory Sensitivities

Chapter 7:
Sensory Sensitivities

Early in my career, I understood the term 'sensitivities' to refer to one's emotions – a sensitive person was more easily upset or affected by difficult or unpleasant situations. Later, when I was diagnosed with multiple allergies, the word sensitivity came to mean the likelihood of an intolerance to certain foods. Nowadays, among professionals, sensitivities refer to heightened responses to inputs from the five physical senses – in other words, sensory sensitivities, which is the term I shall use throughout this chapter and the rest of the book to avoid confusion.

A word of caution before I continue: sensory sensitivities of the kind we're discussing in this book are present from birth. If someone finds they have sensory sensitivities developing as a phenomenon later in their life, they should always seek out a doctor's advice as this may be a sign of some other issue developing.

The physiological roots of sensory sensitivities are not my area of expertise, and in recent years there have been huge strides in the field of neuroscience that help to document and analyse their origins, leading to many useful books on the subject. I'll be highlighting some of these as we go, along with some recommended reading at the end of the book. What I will do in this chapter is describe how sensory sensitivities present themselves in our bright sparks, and ways in which they can be dealt with.

Sensory sensitivities have long been a subject of folklore in gifted communities. Bright individuals who have spoken with one another previously claimed to possess an unusually heightened sense of smell, to notice certain flavours others might miss or to be able to listen and absorb several different voices simultaneously. Until recently, however, there was no reliable way to prove or disprove those kinds of claims. We all experience the world uniquely, and for that reason, those who spoke of enhanced senses of smell or hearing were often dismissed as being either boastful or simply mistaken about the uniqueness of their perceptions.

Now, at last, articles and academic papers like *Neuroscience of Giftedness: Greater Sensory Sensitivity* (Duncan, Goodwin, Haase and Wilson) and *Encountering the Gifted Again, for the First Time* (Jacobsen) have explored the science underpinning sensory sensitivities. The folklore has become fact.

It's worth mentioning that, at this point in time, sensory sensitivities are not classified as a disability. That may change in the future once more research has been undertaken and more proof has been accrued but, for now, sensory sensitivities as we understand them do not meet the criteria that classifies a disability. (Under the 2010 Equality Act, a person is disabled if they have a physical or mental impairment that has a 'substantial' and 'long-term' impact on their ability to perform daily tasks and activities. The 2014 Equality Act added 21 birth conditions to that definition, but a high intellect is not among their number.)

As gifted individuals, many of us grow up and learn to deal with our sensory sensitivities, taking action on a daily basis to minimise triggers and uncomfortable situations in the same way that someone who suffers from hay fever will take antihistamines and carry tissues with them when pollen levels are high. Here are some of the common sensory sensitivities and how to cope with them:

Visual Sensitivities

Visual sensitivities can include a dislike of bright lights, certain colours or visually busy environments. Even in a sound sleep, I am hyperaware of any beam of light that sneaks past the curtains or through the crack in a door that's even slightly open. The minute it touches my face, I'm awake in an instant. Likewise, when we're out and about we might notice the tiny details of what someone is wearing or the minute stain on their collar, individual flowers in a garden or the tiny spider lurking in the corner of the bathroom. I make use of this capacity to capture fine detail when I'm teaching the children at my workshops to draw. Once they're used to studying what's in front of them rather than drawing from their mind's eye, it's remarkable how much artistic confidence they gain.

Dealing with the difficulties of visual sensitivities can be quite straightforward. If bright light is the issue, wearing dark or tinted glasses can help. In the summer I prefer to sleep with an eye mask (the sort they give you on aeroplanes) to help block out tiny light sources from waking me up. During your daily life, if you find that the scene before you is so busy or complex as to be overwhelming, try closing your eyes for a few seconds as long as it's safe to do so. If not, try to avert your eyes to focus on something small or close at hand.

Aural Sensitivities

There are a few noises that almost everyone finds intensely grating. Chalk squeaking on a blackboard will set most people's nerves on edge, for instance, but those with sensory sensitivities can be disturbed by far more subtle sounds that go unnoticed by many other people. People chewing, whispering or even breathing can be enough to cause irritation. I've worked with several bright sparks who find the noise of a pencil writing on paper to be highly distracting. One little girl I know finds the sound of air hand dryers deeply unpleasant.

When most people are in a social situation, such as a party with many intermingled conversations, they learn to filter out the conversations they don't wish to actively participate in. They might even think they're not perceiving them at all, at least until someone across the room mentions their name and their attention immediately snaps to the speaker. Those with sensory sensitivities have no such filter. They're tuned into every conversation, all the time, and focusing on a single person can be incredibly difficult against such a cacophony.

The students I work with are normally delighted to find they're not the only ones who are like this, and that others find the same kinds of noises as aggravating as they do. On the plus side, being tuned in to multiple conversations can be invaluable for monitoring a classroom or managing several groups.

To deal with aural sensitivities, one quick and easy solution is to purchase gel earplugs from your local pharmacy. While these don't block out all sound, they do mute the more minor irritating noises and help to lessen the impact of loud, unexpected ones. As another plus, they're almost undetectable, meaning they don't tend to draw comment at work or school – I know two or three of my bright sparks use them regularly during their lessons. At home, I like to use a silent keyboard and mouse and wear soft-soled shoes around the house.

Where possible, find a reason to move away from any noise that's causing you discomfort. If the sound of somebody chewing starts making me want to throw things, I find an excuse to leave the room – it's not their fault that I'm hypersensitive to sounds!

Tactile Sensitivities

I'm sure we've all experienced uncomfortable clothing at some point – trousers that are too tight, straps that dig into our shoulders, or badly-sized shoes pinching and rubbing at our feet. As with sight and sound, sensitivity to touch can be greatly increased in gifted individuals, with younger bright sparks experiencing this most intensely. These are just a few of the common issues reported by members of my parents' group:

"He hates anyone touching his ears, and hair washing is a major challenge. He will scream and put his fingers in his ears."

"Often complains about labels in clothes hurting."

"He can't stand his nails being cut."

A dislike of certain textures, like velvet or nylon, are also common. When my son was small he refused to walk barefoot across sand; nowadays he despises any form of sauce or similar foodstuff on his face. The list of tactile sensitivities can sometimes seem endless – hair accessories, shoes and socks, your own hair touching the back of your neck, and so on. The only upside is that you tend to be more receptive to pleasurable touching and will enjoy being hugged, holding hands or having your hair brushed.

I've never found a quick fix for tactile sensitivities other than 'positive shopping', where you stock up on those fabrics and other items that don't trigger discomfort. Avoidance is also a useful tactic, but there are times in this life when it's simply not possible to steer clear of unpleasant stimuli. School uniforms can be a big issue – you can get away with flexible dress when children are very young but having to ring your child's school to explain that they won't be attending in uniform because they only wear baggy clothing is another matter entirely.

As an adult, what if your job requires you to wear a particular outfit or piece of safety gear? Weddings, funerals and other formal events all have dress codes. Cognitive Behavioural Therapy (CBT) can help with sensory issues, but it requires support from parents to be successful. Thinking outside the box can sometimes provide an answer to clothing problems – wearing a soft cotton T-shirt underneath a stiff, itchy school shirt, for example. If you need a suit, talk to a tailor and see if it can be adjusted in ways that make it more bearable. At the same time, look for ways to build up your resilience, adapting your behaviour by telling yourself that you can manage the discomfort for a short while and your reward will be collapsing into comfortable clothing when you get home.

Olfactory Sensitivities

I have a powerful sensitivity to smell. Our house is set back 20 metres from the pavement and, even with the doors and windows closed, I can tell if someone's walking past smoking a cigarette. When my husband first came over from America he was perplexed that I would only drink bottled water and – being of an inquiring mind – wanted to test if my dislike of tap water was genuine or if I was just being fussy. While I was out of the room, he procured two identical glasses and filled one from my bottle and the other from the tap, inviting me to taste them. I didn't need to taste; sniffing the contents of each glass was enough for me to correctly identify which was the bottled water.

Having a highly sensitive sense of smell can be a double-edged sword. As a cat owner, I can tell within seconds if a litter tray has been used (or misused) anywhere in the house. I know instantly if food is burning or if the gas hob hasn't been turned off properly. Conversely, plenty of parents tell me about children whose response to odours is so extreme that exposure makes them physically sick. Certain food smells – chlorine in swimming pools or an open wheelie bin – can all induce similarly intense reactions.

Coping with a sensory sensitivity to smells can be hard, but it's not impossible. If the smell is localised, avoidance is usually the best answer, but you can also resort to a trick used by humans around the world for centuries – masking the smell with another, more pleasant one. If you or your child know of a scent you find pleasant, like a perfume or oil, soak a handkerchief with that substance and keep it in a water-tight wrapping or container in your bag or pocket. If you come into contact with an unexpected or unpleasant smell, you can then cover your mouth and nose with the hanky until the alien odour, whatever it may be, has passed.

Gustatory Sensitivities

More commonly known as taste! This type of sensory sensitivity – where food textures or flavours are the problem – can make life difficult not just for the individual but for their family, too. To be clear, though, while babies will eat just about anything you give them, there comes a point when all children get picky about their foods. It's also very common to hate something as a child that you find delicious as an adult, and vice versa.

For safety's sake, should your child gag when eating a particular food, you should check that there's no accompanying rash, facial swelling or breathing difficulties. Food allergies are becoming more and more common and aren't always identified right away. As a child, every single time I was forced to eat sprouts I would be sick and then sent to my room for being fussy. Decades later, it took three weeks of double-blind testing in a hospital to both save my life and confirm that I was suffering from a raft of life-threatening food allergies, including to sprouts and the whole brassica family.

When dealing with lifelong sensitivities, however, it's most common to hear from parents whose children react badly to a particular texture of food. In this case, avoidance of those foods works best. What concerns me more is when I hear about children who won't enter a room if a food is there, or that two foods on the same plate must not be allowed to touch. That's not sensory sensitivity, it's a behavioural trait more typical of a child with ASD. With time and appropriate support, that kind of behaviour can normally be modified or quashed altogether.

In Summary

This brings us back to the concept of resilience, and it won't be the last time you see me mention it! While it's unfortunate that our bright sparks have to face these kinds of sensory sensitivities on top of all the other challenges they cope with daily, others in the world are suffering from famine, abuse and pain. It's important that we, as parents and caregivers, help our gifted children to understand their sensitivities and how to overcome them through tenacity, courage and making good use of their high intellect to spot problems on the horizon and avoid them. If we don't, the long-term prospects are too sad to consider.

Chapter 8

Adolescence

Chapter 8:
Adolescence

Being a teenager is tough. There are countless forms of media reminding us of that fact every day. Some of them are tongue-in-cheek (TV comedy-dramas like *The Inbetweeners* or *Kevin and Perry*) while others are more sympathetic, and there are plenty of TED Talks and guide books that warn parents of the ticking teenage time bomb lurking upstairs. Their message is always the same – adolescence is a difficult time for everyone, no matter who they are or where they come from.

I briefly mentioned awareness bubbles when discussing the social challenges faced by our bright sparks, so let's explore this concept in more detail. Awareness bubbles are a way of visualising how much of the world around us we're able to meaningfully perceive and relate ourselves to at any given time. When we're infants the bubble is tiny – practically skintight. As tots, dropping a toy to the ground is enough to remove it from our perception, and we rely on our caregiver to hand it back when we decide we want it again, even if it's still lying nearby.

As we mature and develop, our awareness bubble begins to expand, but this process takes time. Even if you don't have children of your own, you might have witnessed a toddler who, having been told not to do something by an adult, moves a few feet across the room in order to commit the misdeed. They then appear utterly baffled when their carer, who was watching them the whole time, swoops in to tell them off. Surely grown-ups must possess some sort of magic powers that allow them to know the unknowable!

Further growth and development ensues and, as our awareness bubbles get larger, we begin to understand that we have a presence in the world and that our actions can alter it. Mum has said we can't have a packet of crisps, but Dad is outside washing the car so we could go and ask him instead… Generally, though, we still care very little about how those parts of the world outside of what we can see and hear might function. The thought that our parents might have had a private conversation about how to respond to our predinner snack requests doesn't occur to us.

Our bright sparks, as we've touched upon previously, have larger awareness bubbles than other children their age. They will hear things on the news or in adult conversations that will trouble them while their peers blot the TV out entirely unless it's showing age-appropriate programming. Bright sparks will be upset if something unpleasant is happening in a far-off corner of the playground, even if it doesn't affect the game they're involved in at all.

When adolescence strikes any of us like a tidal wave of new and alien thoughts and emotions, it coincides with a huge swelling of our awareness bubbles. Suddenly, we're hyper-aware of our weight in the world. Not only do we have the power to affect others in meaningful ways, but other people will be observing our actions – maybe even judging us – whether we like it or not.

All those times we've had thoughts and feelings about the people we encounter now come back to haunt us. We realise that, all along, those around us have been having the exact same kind of thoughts, sometimes about us, and even if we're not there! It feels like everyone is staring and monitoring our every move, right at a time where we can't even trust our own bodies not to betray us.

Now imagine that same fateful time from the perspective of our gifted children, whose awareness bubbles were larger than average and who experience heightened empathy towards others. We've already mentioned that people with high IQs like to be in control of their situation, but how can we possibly control the way we present ourselves to others – which we'd like to be an image of perfection, naturally – when we can't control the pitch of our voice or the spots on our face? When we have sensory sensitivities, the pimple on our forehead is going to feel ten times larger than it actually is, and the smell of our own sweaty bodies might seem overpowering to us. Surely everyone else around us can't help but notice us as strongly as we're noticing ourselves?

Chapter 8: Adolescence

At this stage in their lives, it's common for bright teens to take even a mild rebuke from an adult authority figure, like a teacher, incredibly seriously – it's confirmation of all their new doubts and fears about themselves. The most common response to this sudden bombardment of embarrassment and unease is to withdraw to a place of safety and isolation, which can often be their own bedroom.

It can also mean disappearing off outside for long periods of time. When teenagers don hoodies and slink away to lurk around an industrial estate or in the local woods, it's common to assume that they must be up to no good. Chances are, though, they're just looking for somewhere where it doesn't feel like there's a spotlight constantly shining down on them from on high.

The teenage stereotypes in sitcoms are even more accurate when it comes to gifted teens, whose personalities can completely transform almost overnight. Extroverted youngsters who used to love to communicate become shy, silent youths whose preferred method of communication with their families is the text message or, if you're lucky, a monosyllabic grunt. During this time, their behaviour will swing backwards and forwards between adult and childlike needs. One day they might choose to build a fort in their bedroom as they did when they were younger; the next, it's been torn down to make room for the soon-to-be-famous rock band they're starting with their friends.

They might have been top of the class, but there's no coming top in adolescence. Many gifted children, even the ones who have been happy and motivated at school up until this point, will find that this new onslaught of social pressures transform the classroom into an incredibly stressful place filled with unknown pitfalls. Some may start skipping certain classes or even refuse to attend school altogether. As one young woman tearfully told me, "I used to be so good in school, the teachers loved me. I don't know where that person is any more." Our bright sparks are far from oblivious to the drastic personality shifts they're undergoing, but they're unable to express how the changes feel or even to rationalise them.

It should go without saying that every child is different, but generally speaking, young girls tend to cope somewhat better with being bright than boys of the same age, partially because they tend to be both more sociable and more compliant when adults tell them to do something. Unfortunately, the same cannot be said of adolescence, which is made all the more difficult because it arrives earlier in their lives.

Furthermore, girls can often feel pressure to hide or suppress their intellect when they hit their teenage years, a time when boys continue to be defined by their talents and accomplishments but girls are pushed more towards defining themselves by behaviour and personality. Suddenly, maybe for the first time in their lives, being the cleverest one in the room feels instinctively like a bad thing.

When faced with this maelstrom of emotions and alien sensations, some children may express negative thoughts about themselves and their place in the world. Some of those might go onto expressing more distressing behaviours, such as alluding to self-harm. In those circumstances, parents should be aware that help and advice is at hand from a number of sources – your GP is a good place to start.

As scared as the teenager may feel about the changes happening within and around them, this can be an equally terrifying time for anyone sharing a home with them, particularly parents or caregivers. Tried and tested tactics for giving comfort and support can suddenly result in screaming matches and verbal abuse. When it comes to maintaining discipline and order, all bets appear to be off.

As adults, it can be hard for us to think back to our own adolescence with clarity. We tend to remember some periods of our lives more clearly than others, and it's quite common for time and distance to cloud memories of our own upbringing. Even if we recall being sulky or introverted teens, we tend to forget the intensity of the emotions that were churning within us as our hormones ran riot. Even for the brightest individual, this is not a rational time of life.

Instead, parents should realise that the expanded awareness bubble their offspring now possesses extends to them. Probably for the first time, they are being viewed not as the god-like beings that swooped down upon toddlers out of nowhere, nor as infinitely knowledgeable oracles who can fix any problem, but as flesh and blood human beings who have their own flaws – they can get emotional, can be deceived, and don't have all the answers right when they're needed most.

It's important to remember that adolescence is, trite as the term may be, a 'phase', even if it feels closer to eternity. Teenagers will eventually move through these years and into adulthood, as surely as the sun shall rise. As young adults they won't completely resemble their childhood nor their teenage selves; rather, they'll be a fusion of the qualities we've helped them develop throughout their lives, and that includes their high intelligence. One day, you and they will be able to look back on their adolescence together with the benefit of hindsight, and wonder what all the fuss was about.

On top of the other challenges we've discussed so far in the book – physical, emotional, social and sensory sensitivities – the looming spectre of adolescence can make it appear as though our bright sparks, and the adults around them, will have to face many obstacles on the road to adulthood. It seems fundamentally unfair that those children in a position to be creative and brilliant find their natural potential hampered by hurdles that must be overcome. The old adage that life isn't always fair rings true no matter how bright you are.

The solutions we've looked at so far have been in response to specific issues that commonly crop up in the lives of those with high intelligence, like having trouble falling asleep. In the second part of the book we'll look at the broader picture; dealing with everyday existence as a gifted child and working towards a bright, positive future, while laying down some groundwork to ensure that our bright sparks don't stumble later in life. We'll start by taking a look at four rules I consider to be of paramount importance, and how they apply to life at home, school and beyond.

Chapter 9

The Four Rules for Success

Chapter 9:

The Four Rules for Success

Slightly over a decade ago, I was fortunate enough to be asked to speak at British Mensa's Annual Gathering, being held in Chester that year, on the subject of giftedness. The audience was made up of Mensans of all ages and from all walks of life. I gave a very early version of the presentation I use in today's seminars, then left some time at the end for questions and discussion. The conversation came around to higher education, and I asked the group – roughly 50 people – how many of them had been to university. All of them raised their hands.

Next, I asked how many of the group had finished university, coming away with a qualification. This time around, fewer than half of them raised their hand. I was astounded to think that institutions that were supposedly meant to nourish and grow the talents of our very brightest individuals were failing to create meaningful connections with those who had potential to excel, and wanted to know why. As our discussion continued, four main causes began to present themselves as answers.

What I learned on that day, followed by the research and additional reading I undertook as a result of the experience, formed the basis for what I call my Four Rules for Success. They are as follows:

The Four Rules for Success	
Learn how to **study**	Learn how to **fail**
Learn how to **mix with other bright people**	Learn how to **become well rounded**

Sticking to these rules from a young age is important, not just for helping our bright sparks through university, if that's their chosen path, but also when dealing with many aspects of the adult world – it just so happens that higher education is the first time many of these problems present themselves. Let's look at each of the rules in turn, the problems they're designed to tackle, and why those problems might lead to real issues in later life if they're not addressed.

Rule 1: Learn How to Study

Many people would be surprised to learn that, while our most intelligent children tend to begin their schooling seated comfortably at the head of the class, it's probably not a position they'll hold throughout their education. If given the opportunity, they'll excel at primary school and, at secondary school, they'll likewise tend to be at or near the top of their group. When it comes to A-levels, however, it can be quite common to see a wobble: a time when their results aren't quite as outstanding. That wobble increases as the first marks for university coursework and exams arrive.

For much of their lives, our bright sparks have achieved high marks without ever really having to work for them. Instead, they've used their intellects to easily store and recall information that other students have struggled to commit to memory or, failing that, they've relied on mental agility to effectively 'wing it' through tests. In primary and secondary education, where exams tend to focus either on raw literacy and numeracy or on the regurgitation of facts, it's a strategy that's allowed them to flourish.

Teachers can struggle to get their brightest students to 'show their working' in lessons like maths or science. From the student's point of view, it's a tedious and unnecessary waste of time to write out every step of the calculations, because writing is slow and isn't as fun as solving the problem in your head. Besides, if the answer's correct, what does it matter?

Unfortunately for our gifted offspring, the answer – at least in higher education – is that it matters quite a lot. A-level and university qualifications aren't simply a matter of knowing the correct answers. They're designed to teach critical analysis, requiring students to form their own conclusions and, crucially, to justify them. In other words, it's all about showing your work.

Students who are near the centre of the intellectual bell curve have had no choice but to learn how to do this as part of their studies. They've always needed to expand an algebraic equation on paper, step by step, because there's too much to juggle in their brains. The same goes for long division, or working hard to memorise all the Shakespearian quotations that might be useful in an English exam. It doesn't mean the kind of essay writing required by higher education courses comes easily to them, of course, but they at least have a firm grounding in taking a methodical, rigorous approach to their coursework that our bright sparks can lack. What happens next brings us to our second rule…

Rule 2: Learn How to Fail

Let's recap: our gifted offspring have arrived at university, comfortably confident that their intellect will see them coast through their new classes, and then they get their first essay back from their lecturer, only to find that their unfamiliarity with the kind of study that was expected of them has cost them points. Not only is the score low, it's catastrophically low by their perfectionist standards, maybe even one of the lowest marks they've ever received. They don't know that very few people receive a pass mark on their first essays, of course, nor would it provide them any consolation in that moment. It doesn't matter how others have performed, because it never has; what matters is that they believe they have failed to excel.

This shock to the system causes them to ask a very searching question. What if they're not as smart as everyone's been saying they are, at least compared to the strangers that now surround them? Next comes the overthinking. If they don't have the intellectual fortitude to make it through university, what does that mean for their career prospects, long-term happiness and everything they've been dreaming of doing with their lives?

We saw in the last chapter how badly our sense of self-worth can be shaken during our teenage years, and most of us arrive at university in the last lingering stages of adolescence. As if this weren't enough to leave us feeling seriously disoriented in a brand new environment, receiving an essay mark that's leagues below what we're accustomed to only serves to add to our worries and doubts. In our minds, we're suddenly not as clever as everyone thinks we are, and the score we just received all but proves it.

Rule 3: Learn to Mix with Other Bright People

How will most of the other students be dealing with their first, disappointing university essay marks? It's likely that many will return to their Halls of Residence or head out to the pub, disheartened but experienced enough to know that their friends and family will be there to support them and offer advice. As they chat with their new study groups and roommates they'll likely learn that almost everyone gets a low grade on their first essay and the result won't feel so bad.

As we've discussed elsewhere, one common side-effect of high intelligence is an unfortunate emotional immaturity that arises when we don't spend enough time learning to practise play. I notice this a lot in my workshops when my group of 10 and 11-year-olds get together at breaks. Their level of play, the amount of giggling and the games they choose, tends to be what you'd expect from 7 or 8-year-olds thanks to their limited experience socialising. On one occasion, two boys went and hoarded the entire supply of the favoured Happy Cube toys for themselves. They didn't do this maliciously; they just intended to make use of them all eventually and hadn't considered that they should be sharing with the other children.

Not only will our gifted university students have more trouble socialising when they arrive on campus, they most likely won't see much of a need to do so, preferring to fall back on solitary pursuits instead. By doing so, they miss out on a vital lifeline during this very difficult time. Even worse, they might feel the need for companionship, but lack the knowledge or experience to go about making the relationships they need to flourish. Just because you're surrounded by other bright people, it doesn't mean you'll automatically make friends.

Rule 4: Learn to be Well Rounded

In Chapter 6 we touched upon what might happen to Ella if she establishes a self-identity that pivots around being 'the clever one'. If your self-worth is tied to your perception of your own intelligence, you can unwittingly develop a very fragile ego. Universities, as you quickly learn from browsing the Fresher's Fayre or hanging out in the student union, are packed to bursting with very smart people, many of whom excel in fields very different from your own interests.

With a lack of study skills and a low test score having already damaged your self-confidence, it's only natural to ask yourself "If I'm not the cleverest one in the room, then who exactly am I?" If bright sparks like Ella learn to receive praise by reciting their times tables or knowing all the words to a song, then they won't have been receiving other kinds of praise: that they are kind, funny, considerate and fun to be around. Worse still, having seen that other children receive those kinds of praise, the Ellas of the world have grown up assuming that they are not kind, funny, or pleasant company – they're just clever.

When they make the jump to school, other children start unwittingly to help foster this identity with their own comments, asking for help with homework or why you're so clever, rather than asking you to play or what TV shows you like. If circumstances cause gifted students who have had this kind of upbringing to ask themselves what other qualities they possess beyond intelligence, they often draw a blank. This is why it's so important, from a young age, to praise and encourage all aspects of our gifted youngsters' personalities, not just the precocious parts. Sooner or later, they'll need to fall back on their other qualities.

Think about occasions where success didn't come easily. How many would also help you become a better-rounded individual? Pick three and think of ways you could work one or more of them into your routine.

Reaching your daily step count, nurturing a potted plant or sketching a quick drawing are all examples of activities that can be worked at each day in-between your normal tasks.

In Summary

University can provide the perfect storm of circumstances that will severely shake the confidence of our bright sparks. All at once they've found themselves lacking vital study skills, unable to use their natural intellect to excel, surrounded by those who easily match their abilities and cast adrift in a crowd of people who already seem to be fitting in with one another. Given all of this, perhaps it shouldn't be so surprising that so many of the Mensa members who attended my talk had chosen to withdraw from university entirely rather than face, perhaps for the first time, what seemed to be insurmountable challenges.

Ultimately, though, the real world is going to confront our gifted children with these same challenges sooner or later. Dropping out of university won't save them from potentially failing at something where they can't coast by on their intelligence, such as learning to drive. They will one day encounter someone who runs rings around them intellectually and, of course, will have to learn to develop their social skills in order to function in the adult world – renting a house, buying a car, dealing with a noisy neighbour and so on.

By following the four rules – learning to study for those times when intellect alone is not enough, learning how to cope with and learn from failures, learning the value of social skills and how to deploy them and, above all, learning to appreciate oneself as a well-rounded individual with many positive traits – all of us can become better equipped to deal with the life that lies ahead of us. Parents, caregivers and teachers are, of course, a fundamental part in this process, especially when our bright sparks are growing up. Next, we'll look at all the ways they can help.

Chapter 10

Parenting
Bright Sparks

Chapter 10:

Parenting Bright Sparks

Long before the rise of parenting manuals, child development specialists, YouTube video guides and the television, parents were having – and successfully raising – children. Despite the many threats and hazards faced by our cave-dwelling ancestors, we were able to flourish as a species, raising our offspring to adulthood before looking on as they did the same with their own children. Parents in centuries past, enduring difficult circumstances of their own, nurtured progenies who went on to find their place in history: children we know today as William Shakespeare, Leonardo da Vinci and Marie Curie. Why, then, is it now so commonplace for parents to second-guess their own instincts and choose to seek help and advice from afar? What's changed?

In truth, a great many things – changes fuelled by the industrial revolution and the new form of society it produced. Firstly, the cultural expectations placed upon us and our children are far more demanding. So-called 'first-world' nations require that our offspring are educated for many years and to a higher standard than ever before. They're expected to be good communicators, possess a robust social conscience and be willing to fit in with everyone around them, all while being self-sustaining and independent.

Secondly, our government has become entrenched in how we raise our young. The details of our children's health, diets and education are dictated by politicians at Westminster. The behaviour of parents is legislated and there are rules about how we must interact with our children – rules we are supposed to be mindful of even though they can sometimes seem to change on a whim or contradict one another.

Thirdly, we are now a people on the move. Until fairly recently, members of a family tended to live as a group. Rich and poor alike had family homes or lived physically close at hand. Children would mature into adults and go on to raise their own offspring supported by a nearby network of grans and granddads, aunts and uncles, siblings, cousins and lifelong neighbours, many of whom were within easy walking distance.

Few parents would have found themselves in the situation that many do now – raising a child in essential isolation for the sake of a job or an affordable home, far away from family members and surrounded by strangers. The tools we turn to in the absence of help from our friends and relatives can only do so much. A book cannot babysit, and no TV Supernanny will appear to soothe your teething baby when you're facing your third night without sleep. I believe that parents are under more pressure now than ever before.

The advent of child psychology has also drastically altered how we think about childcare. The prevalence of a 'right way' to raise a family has had profound consequences for children and parents alike. For example, the Victorian creed 'spare the rod, spoil the child' was common wisdom until post-war research showed that other cultures were able to produce compliant children without any use of violence. (Tobin, Wu and Davidson 1989.)

At the same time, psychologist John Bowlby's research on post-war children who had been raised in orphanages found that looking after a child's physical health and intellectual needs was not enough. Bowlby (1988) stated that without the 'mothering' aspects of child rearing – touching, proximity, shared attention, play and so on – society would produce damaged adults who were lacking in the social skills they sorely needed.

Today, we know that leaving a child regularly to 'cry it out' can result in them being distrustful of others, lacking in confidence and being overly self-reliant. We also know that the traditional mother figure does not have to provide this kind of care exclusively – any significant other who takes on the role of the main carer will help the child form a secure attachment bond.

What's important is that parents know it's okay to slip up sometimes. In the 1960s, paediatrician Donald Winnicott did much to promote the notion of 'good enough' mothering (Winnicot 2000). He asserted that being a 'perfect' parent could actually hinder development as, if the child never became uncomfortable, bored or sad, they would never learn to deal with these things and so become an adult that lacks tolerance and resilience!

Likewise, siblings do not always get on. That's okay! Children have different temperaments and different needs at different times of their lives. You cannot force your children to be best buddies, but developing the life skills to work with and around each other in the same home will serve them well in the adult world.

What I want to stress is that there's no such thing as a perfect parent. Everyone makes mistakes, but as long as the majority of your parenting is good enough to ensure the child knows that they're loved and supported, and the child has a strong sense of who they are, they will thrive.

The Golden Rule

Before we even think about discussing the needs of the children, I'd first like to help establish one more golden rule. You can think of it as sitting at the centre for the Four Rules of Success, and it will help make any parent's life far more manageable if they keep it in mind. It should be obvious, but in busy day-to-day life it's remarkable how easy it is to forget it!

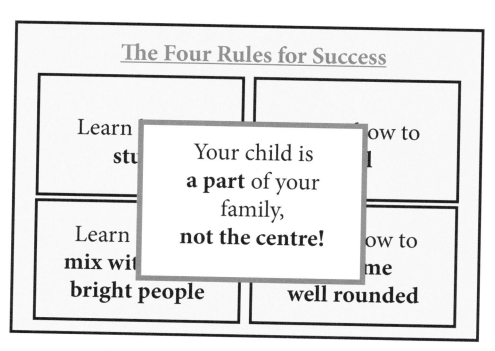

The Four Rules for Success

Learn ... stu...

...ow to ...l

Learn ... mix wit... bright people

Your child is **a part** of your family, **not the centre!**

...ow to ...me well rounded

By being mindful of and sticking to this rule you can help vastly reduce the stress of home life for all concerned. To aid in that, there are three simple things you can do:

1. Make time for your partner

When you and your significant other first got together, you became the centre of each other's worlds. Children were supposed to enhance your relationship, not subsume it. If you don't have one already, put a date night into your schedule and make sure that you stick to it. Make time for one another, whether that's a trip to the cinema or the local café. If you don't have any free babysitting services nearby (more commonly known as family) then hire someone that you know you can trust.

If you can't manage a weekly appointment, go for fortnightly. Even a monthly date night is better than nothing at all. While you're out, talking about your offspring should be taboo. You used to have other things to talk about before children arrived, after all, and this is about nurturing the relationship between the two of you. You'll be stronger as a unit, particularly when your child goes through their phase of trying to play you off against one another.

2. Make time for you

If you as a caregiver are stressed, anxious, overtired or unwell then you cannot parent effectively. You need to build 'me time' into your routine to take care of yourself. Speaking personally, that was a regular two-hour slot on Sunday mornings where my son's father took charge. I'd soak in the bath, do my nails and hair and make myself feel human again. For you it could be going for a run, having a lie-in or engaging in your favourite hobby without the threat of interruption.

3. Make time out for the family

Most children are born into a family unit: two or more adults, possibly other children and maybe some pets, too. When you're all sharing one space things can get fraught, especially at the end of the day, so pick a time to be apart and make it a daily ritual. During this time everyone spends, say, 30 minutes on their own. At some time that suits your routine (before or immediately after dinner is ideal) everyone goes to a separate room to read, draw, wash the dishes, do their homework... The list of possible activities is endless, but the psychology is simple. You've each had a busy day, probably with very little let-up, and you each need a break from other people – time to gather your thoughts and have a mental rest.

Challenges Parents Face

Being the parent or caregiver of a bright spark can feel very isolating. When waiting to collect their children at the school gates or after a party, other parents will discuss their offspring's achievements and milestones. If you try that, it can sound like you're boasting. Elsewhere, other members of your family who might not have exceptionally able children can take offence if yours is always the main topic of conversation.

In these situations, you may need to take the lead. Plan the responses you'll give in advance when subjects of accomplishment and progress come up, and make sure that you stress all of your child's qualities (particularly when they're in earshot) and not just the intellectual ones. It's also okay to talk about some of your child's weaker areas – it makes them seem more human to other people. Whatever your circumstances, I would strongly suggest that you join a support group for parents of gifted children. It's reassuring to know you're not the only parent going through these trials.

It's a common presumption that, as the parent of a bright spark, you must be strapping them to a chair the minute they get home from school and forcing them to recite their times tables, learn Latin or practise the ukulele. The fact that our children are tremendously self-driven will be a detail that eludes most people. We might be considered 'pushy' parents.

Pushy parents are rare, but they do exist, and I'm often asked "Am I a pushy parent?" by worried mums and dads. My answer goes something like this: pushy parents are those who will never be satisfied with their child's accomplishments – no matter what they achieve, it will never be enough. They will take credit for their child's achievements and bask in the reflected attention that their offspring receives. Meanwhile, the child's life will be scheduled to the nth degree, with goals and activities in place to make sure the child is 'making the most' of every waking moment, regardless of what they actually want and the knock-on effect the regimen has upon family life.

I remember one parent who contacted me by phone, explaining that their child had joined Mensa on their third attempt. In order to maximise the child's opportunities, they now worked to a daily schedule. At 5pm, after she'd completed her homework, she was given half an hour's additional study. At 5:30, it was time for 30 minutes of piano practice. At 6pm, it was mealtime, where a topic of debate would be tabled by the father. At 6:30, it was half an hour of a television programme chosen by both parents, and so on. The child was 7 years old, and I asked when in all of this she had time to play. The parent hung up the phone and I never heard from him again.

The fact is, parents of gifted children have no need to go to such lengths – it's slowing our bright sparks down that can be the trouble.

I remember my son racing into the bedroom in the early hours of the morning, four years old and totally enthused. He began to speak at length about 'x', which affected other numbers and there were loads of things you could do with it, even work out problems that were too big for one person's brain! (He'd made his way downstairs and had been watching the Open University lectures again.)

Elsewhere, the ever-present overthinking can cause separation anxiety in gifted children of all ages. When the child can imagine all sorts of dreadful events taking place while their caregiver is absent, it becomes much easier simply not to leave the adult's side. Equally, if the parent is feeling anxious, the child will pick up on this and become anxious themselves – which in turn further heightens the parent's anxiety, leading to an emotional feedback loop which can be difficult to break. Learning to catch yourself overthinking, stand back and 'see the wood for the trees' is an important skill that both parents and children should work to develop.

Note down the ways you've successfully encouraged your bright spark to overcome their separation anxiety and how. You can share these tips with other parents in an online group and learn a few new ones in return.

Sometimes, though, our brilliant little overthinkers can exude confidence. They like to take charge and, if given the opportunity, will wind up running the household with their ideas, demands and preferences. When you're an overwrought parent juggling the needs of work, other family members and so on, sometimes it feels quicker and easier to let them. In the long run, you're not doing your bright spark a favour by allowing this. Emotionally, they still need the security of an authority figure seen to be in control; if you let them rule the roost, you might be setting them up for a fall by leading them to believe that life will always work this way.

There's no doubt that caring for a gifted child is hard work. Their constant worries, questions, and demands for attention can be exhausting. Trouble sleeping, sensitivities and frustrations could make life very difficult – but it doesn't have to be. Next, let's take a look at the many positives, ways of dealing with the demands and the lighter side of living with a bright spark.

Chapter 11

Being Supportive

Chapter 11:
Being Supportive

As parents, we shape our children in all kinds of ways – sometimes just by existing. That said, we also get plenty of chances to act in a manner that helps to keep our bright sparks contented as well as develop resilience, patience and the other social skills they'll need growing up. In this chapter, let's take a look at some useful tips and tricks that a parent can deploy in everyday life.

Make Time for Play

All of us need to play now and then. It's a type of downtime that, whatever form it takes, has been shown to reduce levels of stress and aggression even in adults. For children, it has other benefits too. It can help the mind to process all of the information it's taken in, and – just as importantly – it gives a child time to practise new skills without being under pressure. Play allows them a chance to test out social, emotional and physical ideas about how the world works, and acts as a precursor to learning more complex skills later in childhood.

Play doesn't require expensive toys or manufactured equipment. Watch children around the world kick around a piece of tinfoil in lieu of a football. A stick wrapped in some old rag becomes a doll to play with. How many times have you seen a child receive a new toy only to have more fun playing with the big box it came in? Timeless games like Tag and King of the Castle require only space to race around. I had plenty of jolly times with my son playing Pooh sticks on the bridge near our house. (For the uninitiated, the game comes from A. A. Milne's classic *The House at Pooh Corner* and sees all players drop their chosen stick into flowing water on one side of a bridge. The winning stick is the first to emerge on the other side. There have even been World Championships!)

Play is important for our physical health and mental well-being. It also reduces anxiety in our bright sparks. Simple acts like running as fast as they can, pushing themselves higher on a swing or building a blanket fort are the active, daytime equivalents of the single-focus activities that help them get to sleep. Real play requires focus. Play also helps teach independence, encouraging children to move away from activities directed by adults and occupy themselves.

Although play was once given priority at school, recent years have seen the school day shortened and playtime is an unfortunate casualty of this. Primary schools may have a morning and afternoon recess, but these are shorter than they used to be. At secondary school, there is now a short morning break of 15 minutes or so and a lunchtime that's barely long enough to eat, let alone play. When teaching, I saw many students opt out of lunch so that they had time to play a game of football or practise dance. More than ever, making time for play outside of school should be a priority.

Activity

Note down how much time in a day your child gets to play – that's time they direct themselves and don't have other tasks to complete like getting dressed or eating. How does it compare to their adult-directed time? Could the balance be better?

Variety is Key

Although play is common across the world and the same kinds of games pop up over and over again in different cultures, children aren't born knowing all of the games and activities there are. They learn higher-level play, like the street games I mentioned, both from adults and other children around them. (Basic-level play, in contrast, is something like making a mud pie or running around.)

Our bright sparks need a lot of keeping busy, and they'll keep returning to you to satisfy that need, particularly when they're younger. Running yourself ragged trying to keep them occupied does you no good at all and won't be helpful to them in the long run either, but there are a few ideas you can try:

■ Take their toys, books and so on and divide them up into several boxes, each containing a variety of activities, and bring out a different box each day. A week is a massive amount of time in a child's world so a toy they haven't seen in a few days will be 'as new' to them. Use this toy box as a way to introduce their self-occupying time.

■ When you have chores to do, your child can be nearby. They can be playing, 'helping' you, or you can occupy them in other ways – you could both be singing, or you could tell them a story.

■ Around the house, play I-Spy or, if they're still developing language skills, play the 'What's This?' game. Carry them around the house, point to an object and ask, "What's this?" If they don't know, name the object ("It's a door!") and move onto the next thing. There will come a time when they will instigate the game with you by pointing and asking "Dis?" It's great fun to watch their reaction when, after a few turns, you give a silly answer. ("It's an elephant!")

■ Take them for a short, slow walk outside and look at everything around you. Point out gardens, birds, chimneys and insects. Take a bag along in which to collect leaves, flowers and other interesting things – the child can use them to make a picture or paste them into a scrap book when you get home, which is more self-occupying time.

■ Keep old clothes and shoes in a box for dressing-up games. Save birthday and Christmas cards as the designs can be used for cutting out and making collages.

With school-age children the approach needs to be slightly different. You may have noticed that when your child comes home from school and you ask them what they've done that day, they'll reply that they can't remember. They're not being difficult or trying to keep secrets from you; they really can't remember – at least, not yet.

The multitude of facts, figures, sights, smells and voices that have bombarded their brain all day take time to be processed and sorted into their memory. They can't access them until that's done. Very often you'll find that they'll suddenly tell you about something that happened a few days ago, but then again, you may never know. Allow school-age children to have some downtime to process their day as soon as possible after they get home.

Some of the best games with school-aged bright sparks can be spontaneous. My son and I would have sessions where we could only sing to one another, or speak in rhyme, or begin our sentences with the letter B. Getting the whole family involved in a game can be tremendous fun, and once other members have picked up the idea you can either stand back or continue to join in the fun.

Thinking back to the Four Rules, encourage your child to play with other youngsters. If playing outside isn't possible or safe, then the garden or the house will do, or you can take them to the park. Use the online groups I mentioned as a means to introduce them to other bright sparks, too. Gifted children will enjoy hanging out together at places like museums or exhibitions as well as more formalised activities.

 Think back to your favourite games and activities when you were a child. Try to remember how they were played and what the rules were. Type them up and keep them safe until your child is at an age where they could make use of them. You could also ask friends or family members about the games they played.

Planning Ahead

"Apples don't fall far from their trees," as my friend and colleague Lu likes to say. She's referring, of course, to familial similarities. After my talks, parents of bright children will come up and say they recognised themselves in my descriptions, and there is an excellent chance that if you're the parent of a gifted child, you yourself will possess a high IQ and be prone to many of the same habits, including overthinking.

If that's so, you can put your overthinking tendencies to good use and make your life easier by forward planning, keeping one step ahead of your gifted offspring. Consider a lengthy car trip – a trial for almost any family. When you've got a bright spark in the back constantly asking questions or declaring "I'm bored!" every mile or so, planning ahead can mean the difference between a journey and a nightmare.

Put together a travel pack of activities, but keep it with you and – as with the daily toy boxes I mentioned – don't dole it out all at once. Tried and tested inclusions are sticker books, Happy Cubes, paper and crayons, storybooks, tablets and jigsaws with pieces large enough not to get lost in the depths of a car seat. Books like Jean Marzollo's *I Spy* series were seemingly invented for our bright sparks and one of those given out at the beginning of a journey will keep them going for a while. Make sure they have a tea tray or a large book to lean on.

Every 20 minutes or so, depending upon the age of the child, you can introduce new activities to stave off boredom. Stick to your timings, though – just because something doesn't take your child's fancy is no reason to let them take charge and select what comes next.

Remembering that your child will also be overthinking and anxious if a journey to somewhere unfamiliar is sprung upon them, you can help to alleviate their anxieties if you discuss the trip with them a couple of days ahead of time, so that they have time to think through and process the information.

Let's look at an example using Ella and her family, who are going to see her first pantomime. A couple of days before, Ella's Mum sits down with her: "Ella, we have a treat for you. On Saturday, which is two days from now, we are going to a pantomime. We will travel to Norwich on a bus and go to a theatre. A theatre is a building where plays and other forms of entertainment take place. They are usually quite big and about 2,000 people can go at the same time. At the front of a theatre is a stage, and everyone looks at the stage like they're watching TV. The people who watch sit in rows of chairs, and the chairs are like armchairs but the seats can flip up."

"The actors will all wear funny costumes. When the actors come out onto the stage the lights will go out and we will sit in the dark. That's so we can see the actors more easily. There will be some parts where everyone laughs and parts where everyone gets to shout at the actors. They may go "Boo!" if it's a baddie or shout helpful things if it's a goodie, but none of it is real life – it's like playing pretend. After the pantomime the actors take off their make-up and change back into their everyday clothes. They're all really good friends."

Of course, Ella immediately has questions, but she's asking them at home rather than in a loud voice at the pantomime itself. Giving her advance notice allows her to work through her overthinking, get her anxieties out of the way, and enjoy the pantomime.

Even a visit to a family member can be dealt with in the same way. "Auntie gets upset if anyone touches her ornaments but you are allowed to stand and look at them. When she serves dinner there may be some things that you don't like. If that is so, nobody makes a fuss; we just eat the things we do like and leave the rest." Explaining the social rules of the event ahead of time allows the child time to prepare and reduce their stress levels, prevents awkward moments during the visit and gives them the confidence to attend future events.

Manage Your Spending

It's common for children to drain the bank accounts of their parents, but most manage it by leaving the tap running, accidentally buying 20 apps on an unlocked tablet or, in later life, racking up huge phone bills. On top of these regular misdemeanours, our bright sparks' attentions tend to flit like butterflies from one hobby to another, meaning that they often lose interest and move onto something new after a few weeks. Although you want to be a supportive parent, it can get pretty expensive to finance all of these short-lived fascinations.

I speak from experience here, as someone who struggled to find a quarter-sized violin for her son only to be told by his teacher a few weeks later that he now preferred – and was better at – the piano. Before that, there had been the (thankfully brief) flirtation with the drum kit that served as his Christmas present. We did eventually get a piano, but only after a year of lessons using a cheap electric keyboard convinced us that he'd finally found an instrument he'd stick with.

Be the Adult

As we discussed earlier, awkward questions are a stock-in-trade for our bright sparks. Their natural curiosity combined with overthinking leads them to all sorts of topics, many of which will be age inappropriate. Remember, as when I avoided discussing the birds and bees with my 4-year-old son, it's okay for you, as the adult in the room, to give a bare minimum of information when asked. You could even say "You don't need to know that right now. I'll tell you about it when you're [x] years old." (Always give a specific age. If you elect to say "I'll tell you when you're older" you can look forward to the child regularly asking you if they're old enough to be told yet!)

My son, while holding his newborn cousin on his lap, studied her for a while and then declared "I am 6 years older than my cousin, and I always will be. I shall always be more experienced than her." The same, of course, is true for parents of even the most gifted children. Yes, your bright spark may know more than you about astronomy, the capital cities of the world and so on, but you will always be more experienced than they are. Don't be afraid to tell them so if it's needed in difficult situations. It's a fact that can't be argued with!

Our children are always learning from us, whether they realise it or not. (If you're in the company of a young baby, poke your tongue out a bit and watch the response.) As such, we should remember the importance of modelling behaviour. Even if you don't feel very certain, displaying an air of certainty will make your child feel safe with you. Equally, establishing rules and standards and sticking to them will help to raise a secure child who knows that you can be relied upon. If your child gets angry and shouts at you, it's usually because they trust you implicitly and know that it's safe for them to do so. Moreover, they're still learning about life and will sometimes make bad choices. Treat these mistakes as exactly what they are, mistakes. Talk them over, set things right and then move on.

Finally, take every opportunity you can to have fun with them. Our bright sparks can be fun, loving and excellent company to be with. Focus on the good bits and make plenty of happy memories for you all as you go along, treasuring the time you have together. After all, so much of their childhood is spent away from you at school. Which brings us neatly onto our next subject…

Chapter 12

Examining Education

Chapter 12:
Examining Education

In Chapter 10, I mentioned how modern society places more expectations on our offspring while they're growing up than ever before. For proof of this, we need look no further than the demands placed on the British education system. Two hundred years ago it was enough for most working people to be able to read, write and perform basic arithmetic in order to do their jobs. (These fundamentals are often called 'the three Rs' and nowadays are taken to mean "reading, writing and 'rithmetic", though the precise origin and meaning of the phrase has been lost to time. If only they'd taught it in school…)

As occupations have become increasingly diverse and technical, however, we are required to have mastered 'people skills' and cultural knowledge alongside earning our vocational and academic qualifications. It is expected that both parents and schools will have their part to play in teaching these. Citizenship, computer studies and science are all part of a modern education.

Following the 1944 Education Act, the modern model of schooling was developed at a time when the 'production line' model was peaking in industry, and was conceived along much the same lines. You toss children in at one end of the system to move along at a uniform speed, different people work on them at set times, and a well-rounded, educated young adult topples off the conveyor belt at the other end.

This is an oversimplified metaphor, but the truth is that it's an approach which works pretty well for most children. Unfortunately, if you learn at a different rate to others, your passage through the system is far from ideal – our square pegs have a habit of getting lodged in the machinery.

The specifics of the education doled out by the system – what gets taught and when, how long for and to what depth – are at the mercy of whoever is currently in power. Changes in curriculum, exams and inspection are prescribed by cabinet ministers and, as we saw at the start of the book, attitudes towards gifted children have been especially whimsical over the years. There has rarely been provision to dislodge a stuck square peg from the assembly line, at least for very long.

Attitudes towards how we educate our children have shifted greatly over the last century, but that's nothing compared to changes in the ways we educate our teachers. When all your students needed to learn was the three Rs, the most a qualified teacher needed to be was literate, numerate and handy with a cane to keep the students in line. Twice in the 20th century, post-war Britain drafted in ex-servicemen to replace its depleted supply of teachers.

As more sophisticated skills were required of our workers, teachers needed to be increasingly well-educated themselves in order to prepare their charges for the adult world. Teaching became a vocation: a job for life that required a significant amount of time and devotion. Teachers would spend four years learning their craft alongside working towards their degree. They studied both the philosophy and psychology of education, as well as undertaking 'Professional Studies' – in short, the role was taken extremely seriously.

When the country's economy took a hit, so too did the money available for teacher training. Although there still are three- or four-year undergraduate teacher training courses, the majority of primary school teachers and all secondary school teachers now qualify by taking a post-degree course (known as a 'Post Graduate Certificate of Education', or PGCE) that takes just a single year to complete. Furthermore, with a shortage of teachers and the troubling tendency of those who qualify to stay in the job for just a few years before moving on, the education system has instigated a 'Teach First' route into the profession, whereby trainee teachers study part-time alongside working in a classroom.

To be absolutely clear, I am in no way criticising modern teachers – in fact, I really feel for them. They're being placed in front of a class of children having received only the most basic classroom management training, as opposed to the skills I was taught that allowed me to keep teaching for over 40 years. By failing to invest in proper training, I believe that we're burning out and driving away some potentially brilliant teachers. In fact, I've watched it happen.

As far as Special Educational Needs is concerned, I've heard from PGCE students that they're lucky if they get a day or two learning about the subject. When the topic is covered, gifted and talented education gets a mention and then the conversation concludes by discussing pushy parents. Currently, the government does not consider that exceptionally able children have special educational needs. Instead, teachers are fed misinformation about gifted children and, sadly, that stereotype of the pushy parent masterminding their development is often supported by mainstream media. Who are they to say otherwise?

Those same press outlets seem to delight in running stories about 'bad teachers' and 'low standards' in schools. They set parents' expectations higher than ever while encouraging a culture that prefers to criticise, rather than support, the teachers in whose hands their children are placed every day. It's important to remember that teachers are people too, with families and homes of their own. Like anyone in any job they get sick, experience traumatic life events and face difficulties away from the classroom.

 Whether you're a parent or not, imagine waking up one morning to discover you have 25 children to parent. How would your approach to dealing with them change compared to raising an only child?

If you took a stab at the activity on the previous page, your first thought might have been how much of your day would be taken up juggling the logistics of childcare – preparing food, doing the laundry and so on. More than that, though, how would your relationship with each of those children be affected? The time you'd have for any one child would be severely restricted, and while you were spending it with them, how would you manage the behaviour of everybody else?

Classroom teachers won't be handling the cooking and cleaning, but they have plenty of responsibilities beyond teaching their charges and keeping them from harm. They must produce rigorous lesson plans and be able to prove to others that every child in the class is making progress. Work will need to be marked and teaching resources prepared. Troublemakers will need to be dealt with while workmen and women, fire drills, power cuts and other unexpected incidents are worked around at short notice.

Given all of that, how much time can we realistically expect teachers to have left for getting to know the children in their class, learning their idiosyncrasies and understanding what they're capable – or not capable – of? Even in primary school, where the teacher and children spend much of their day together, it can be a monumental task. In secondary school, where teachers generally deal with six different groups of children one after another, it's nigh on impossible.

How do teachers survive the day? They rely on the mentality of the production line. The class is spoken to as a single unit and every child is provided with similar work at a similar rate (with only minor variations), dictated by a timetable devised elsewhere. As I said, this approach works well for most children, and it's why classes are grouped together by age – by and large everyone will be developing at the same sort of speed.

Our homes, of course, are not a production line. Within a family unit we can enjoy a level of flexibility in our routines, working to our own individual needs in a way that teachers normally can't. Even in a small nursery group, our bright sparks can have some freedom to stand out from the crowd. In a secondary school class, they may be one of 30 pupils.

We have provided teachers with a square peg: a child who cannot be taught by treating them as part of a single unit. It's easy to fall into the trap of blaming the school for not accommodating our child's unique needs, but doing so within the confines of the classroom is no mean feat. This is especially true given, as we have seen, that a gifted child's development may be ahead in some areas but lagging behind in others.

Lack of training and insufficient time to provide for a gifted child's requirements can colour much of how a teacher deals with our bright sparks when they appear in their classroom, but what about the children themselves? How do they react to being treated as a cog in the educational machine, a very different experience to what's come before? Often the result is a huge discrepancy between how they perform and behave in the classroom to the kind of person they are at home – a phenomenon I call 'The Stranger at School'.

This disparity between how our bright sparks behave at home and at school can often cause conflict between parents and teachers. It takes many forms, but there are three I see with particular frequency:

1. The child loses interest in studying at home but performs really well at school

Personally, this is the outcome I think parents should hope for. Their bright spark is working hard and clearly feels challenged enough by the material they're being presented with during the school day. Why, then, might parents be anxious?

Sometimes it's the shock of the change. If you've lived with a gifted child who's demanded constant stimulation from you all their life, and this suddenly stops, it's only natural to wonder if everything's okay. Have they lost their motivation to learn, or been told not to do extra work at home? Probably not, but it's a good idea to check just in case.

In this scenario, the school can work with the parents by arranging a quick meeting or phone call to discuss how well the child is doing and longer term plans for their education. In return, parents can work with the school by not overdoing the contact. Weekly phone calls are only necessary if there's an evident problem. As long as your child is content and happy to go to school, you need do nothing more than be supportive. What you can do is use that freed-up home time to help develop their social skills with fun and relaxing activities of the kind they don't get to do at school – bearing in mind that many teenagers will be quite affronted if you start trying to schedule their free time.

2. The child continues to study at home but doesn't perform to their potential at school

This is the biggest cause of friction I've seen between home and school. Up in their bedroom or at the family dining table, the child is choosing to spend their time writing fantastic stories, answering GCSE-level maths questions and learning another language. In the classroom they'll scrawl down three or four sentences without punctuation, make mistakes in simple problems and pick the simplest, shortest books they can find to read.

Parents might choose to respond to this by explaining to the teacher that their child is underperforming at school and bring in examples of the work they do at home. The teacher, by contrast, has seen no evidence of this supposed high ability and may act under the assumption that the child is producing work under duress by pushy parents. I consulted one set of parents in this predicament who had been outright accused of doing additional work themselves before trying to pass it off as their child's!

There can be many reasons for this discrepancy. Our bright sparks are, as we should expect, smart enough to know that they can do things the other children can't, and also that being different can lead to isolation and make you a target for bullies. As a result, they deliberately underperform so that they're in no danger of being made to stand in front of the class and be praised or asked to read their work out to the others as a shining example.

Alternatively, they may be underperforming to placate the teacher, doing everything that's asked of them but no more. When my son was young, he whizzed through a piece of homework that his class teacher had told them should take around 30 minutes, and so carried on through the book until his time was up. Her response was to shout at him in front of the class as she now had no more homework prepared.

Another reason is the sensory sensitivities we discussed earlier. I've seen this in action at school while observing classes. Children will tell me that the others in their class are noisy and disruptive, though when I've been in the classroom I've found this not to be the case, witnessing the normal amount of movement and conversation you would expect to find in a productive classroom. To our bright sparks, this minimal noise level is genuinely distracting, especially when you factor in the teacher moving around the classroom, noises from outside, brightly coloured displays on all of the walls…

The solutions to these problems can be straightforward, but often lack the 'quick fix' parents are hoping for. With sensory sensitivities, the aforementioned gel earplugs can help, as can making sure the child sits at the back of the room – ideally in the corner. This immediately halves the number of directions unwanted stimuli can come from. Deliberate underperformance, on the other hand, can be tackled more easily by the teacher than the parents.

3. The child continues to study at home but, at school, they refuse to study altogether

I recall an occasion where I was holding my workshop for 5- to 7-year-olds. It was their first session and so we started with Study Skills, and since all of the children could read I talked them through how to complete SRA cards. (If you're not familiar with these, they're stand-alone cards used for teaching Study Skills.) All was going well until I walked around the room and found that nobody had written down any answers to the questions on the cards.

Several of the children were able to tell me the answers when quizzed, they just hadn't committed their answers to paper. Upon further discussion I learned that each of them only wanted to write down the answer if they were absolutely sure it was correct. They simply could not bear to take the risk of writing down something that might turn out to be incorrect. After many years of working with bright sparks I had anticipated that one or two of them (but by no means all of them) might behave this way, so we shifted gears and the second part of the lesson was spent discussing our old friends, resilience and risk-taking.

The same problem can arise at school – the child can be so mortified at the thought of getting something wrong, particularly in front of the others, that they flat-out refuse to complete any tasks. In the most severe cases this refusal to study will bleed over into their home life, too. Getting over this hurdle is a long-term piece of work that requires cooperation between home and school.

If your child is refusing to study or failing to reach their potential, I would always start by investigating the common causes I've mentioned so far. There is another possibility, but it's one I've deliberately avoided discussing up until now because it's often the first conclusion parents jump to, and they're often incorrect. There is a chance, however, that the school has adopted such a blinkered approach to education that they cannot accept that not all children fit on their production line.

This insistence on a 'one-size-fits-all' approach is to the detriment of children at both ends of the ability scale, and can make school a miserable experience for children as well as leaving them with a poor self-image. I was recently told about one primary school that tested a 6-year-old student who was found to have a reading age of 8 years, 6 months. Their response was to do nothing with this new information, and insist that the child continue to read books that were far too easy for her because that was what the rest of her class were doing.

Likewise, a friend of mine once taught a Year 2 class that included a high-ability child, so she went and borrowed some books from the Year 4 classroom for her to read. She was instructed to stop doing this by the Headteacher, whose rationale was that the child would have nothing left to read by the time she reached Year 6!

Thankfully, schools that adopt this narrow-minded approach are rarer than you might imagine. Most, along with the individual teachers, are willing to help if they can, they just lack the time, knowledge and resources to deal with our bright sparks effectively. When I deliver teacher training courses in schools and explain how to deal with exceptionally able kids without disrupting the rest of the class, it's always lovely to watch light bulbs appear over heads in the room. There are usually more questions than we have time for and many staff stay in touch so that they can continue to ask them.

In Summary

If you have a bright spark, however worried you are about their progress, conflict with the school can and should be avoided. If both parties are able to put aside their preconceptions, manage their expectations and are willing to practise some give and take, there is much that can be done to ensure that our square peg makes it down the processing line and emerges as a well-rounded individual, even if the route they take isn't exactly the same as their peers. In the next chapter, we'll look at the ways parents and teachers can cooperate to smooth out the bumps.

Chapter 13

Support in School

Chapter 13:

Support in School

Supporting a Bright Spark's Education as a Parent

Whether your child was assessed at 2 years old or 10, approaching a new school with the news that they're a bright spark is a conversation that requires diplomacy. Plonking a psychologist's report triumphantly under a teacher's nose at your next Parents' Evening will do little to establish good relations. When I've assessed a child and the results confirm that they're of exceptional ability, I suggest to parents that a low-key approach is best.

If the child is at primary school, I recommend making two copies of the report, each in its own envelope along with a covering letter. One should be marked for the attention of their teacher, the other for the Headteacher. Within the covering letter, explain your willingness to support the school in providing for your bright spark and request a meeting in the coming week or two, where you can discuss how home and school can work together. At secondary school, do the same, but address one copy to their form tutor and another to their Head of Year.

This approach will give the teaching staff time to digest the information, talk to one another and formulate a plan of action that they can then talk over with you at the meeting. Giving them this breathing room will show them that you're not trying to pressure the school – but equally, you're not just going to go away. As we touched upon in the previous chapter, as important as your child is to your family life, to their teacher they will be one of 30 students who all need equal time and attention.

Remember, too, that there's a lot more to school than maths and English, and there will be many lessons where your child is learning at an age-appropriate level along with their classmates. They'll also be picking up a host of other skills without realising it: queueing for and choosing their lunch, sitting quietly as part of a large crowd and bolstering their independence and resilience. There is plenty your bright spark can learn at home, but lots that only school can teach them. Help them stand on their own two feet by accepting that you don't need to know about every single facet of their school day.

Chapter 13: Support in School

When I taught in primary schools, my favourite parents were those who had ensured their child could dress themselves, go to the toilet unsupervised, blow their own noses and eat their lunch without redeploying it as a fashion accessory. If they could use a pair of scissors and tie their shoelaces (not at the same time) that was a bonus. Sadly, we had plenty of students who would arrive being able to do none of those things, and time they could have spent learning about the world was spent teaching them these fundamentals.

Before your child starts secondary school, there are also some very useful skills you can teach them. Show them how to pack a bag properly so they can access and avoid losing or damaging their books and equipment. Tell them what to do if things go wrong. Offer ways of dealing with children they don't like, or who might not like them, and prepare them to deal with older students pointing at them and going "aww!" like they've spotted a toddler during their first few weeks.

When they transition into Year 10, you may need to adjust your responses. As part of the modelling behaviour we spoke about in Chapter 5, where your bright spark will take their cues from you, be prepared to create an atmosphere of trust and support – this time, by virtue of inaction. For the majority of teenagers, gifted or not, education drops to the bottom of their priority list in favour of friendships, relationships, social media and their appearance. Teachers understand this, and are very adept at constantly stressing the importance of getting homework done, not being absent from school, studying for mock exams and so on, all to keep their students as focused on their studies as possible. They begin to pile on the pressure at the beginning of Year 10, starting as they mean to go on for the next two years.

Our bright sparks, however, are well aware of what's expected of them. The additional pressure from teachers to stay on task can be taken too seriously, almost personally, as if their current pace isn't good enough. Barely three or four weeks into the term they'll be trying to juggle homework, coursework and their social lives while remaining convinced that their teachers believe they're underperforming. This is when cracks may begin to show.

On top of this, schools will be sending regular letters or e-mails to all Year 10 parents, reminding them of how important studying is and hoping that they'll reinforce the message. As conscientious parents who may be gifted themselves, it's natural to follow up thoroughly and want to quiz our offspring – are they doing their homework, have they done a revision timetable, and so on. This risks reinforcing the existing misconception; not only does the child believe their teachers think they're underperforming, but apparently now their parents do too. Meltdowns and arguments can ensue, which isn't a nice time for anyone.

If parents want to support their teachers without accidentally fostering a teenage school-refuser, they will need to play their part differently. Take communication from the school with a pinch of salt and realise that it's not really meant for you any more than the dire warnings of exam failure were intended for your child. If your bright spark has worked to earn your trust by being a good student in the past, then trust them now – if they say they're doing all their homework within school hours then they probably are, and school will let you know via individual communication rather than a form letter if there's a genuine problem.

By all means ask your teen how things are going, but not every day. Once a week is enough, and if there are no problems, just let them know that you're there if needed. By showing that you trust them, you'll be alleviating the extra pressure and it will increase their confidence knowing that you're on their side.

If you find your bright spark still wants to keep studying when they get home from a full day of school, try offering them a breadth of activities. It's a big world out there and they can learn to play an instrument, take up a new sport, learn a language or do research into their current obsession.

If they're fixated on academic work, you can make a study box. Fill it with activity books of the sort you get from bookshops and stationers, making sure they're appropriate for the level your child is working at. Next time they complain that school is too easy, point them to the study box and let them get on with it. Don't forget that allowing them time to relax and socialise is as important as their desire to learn. If they're having trouble making friends at school, it's even more important that they have the chance to do so outside of it.

Lastly, you can show your support for the school in other ways – become a parent governor, for instance, or join the PTA. Consider volunteering to help out at events or do some fundraising for new equipment. Actions like these helps convince the school that you and they are on the same team, and both just want what's best for your child.

Next, let's talk about what the school can do to help.

Supporting a Bright Spark's Education as a School

When it comes to being contacted by parents, my busiest time is the first part of each year's autumn term. At this point, expectations that parents have of schools (and vice versa) have not been met, and there may already have been meetings and phone calls. There are two ages of child that particularly seem to struggle with this time of the year.

The first is, as we've touched upon, the Year 10s. I can only stress to teachers that, if you teach any high ability students in Key Stage 4, it is beneficial to take them aside and have a quiet word, explaining that what you are saying to the class as a whole does not apply to them and that you appreciate their hard work and knowledge.

Over the years I've seen too many gifted students crack under the pressure of thinking they're destined to fail their exams. Your task with these bright sparks is to support them in keeping the pressure and their workload manageable so that they actually make it to exam season and get the best results they can.

During 25 years of secondary school teaching, it's no exaggeration to say that I've seen two or three students each and every year who end up refusing to attend school, self-harming or truanting as a result of the pressure. Ultimately, they either took no exams or maybe sat just one or two, a far cry from what they were capable of. Quite apart from their own prospects, think how much rosier the school's exam results would have been if those students were able to get the grades they had the potential to get.

The second-most-common age group that struggle with the autumn term used to be 7- and 8-year-old boys, but over the last couple of years I've found that they've been overtaken by much younger children. Now, more than ever, our bright sparks are struggling to adapt to reception and Year 1 classes. I'm seeing common behaviours present themselves, mostly in 5- and 6-year-old boys:

- Running around the classroom while shrieking

- Having meltdowns with no obvious cause, which lead to running off, hiding, hitting or throwing things

- An inability to stay on task

- An inability to produce work that meets the required level, let alone what they're capable of

- Aggression towards other children

At this point, it's quite natural for the teacher to assume that this behaviour is either the result of poor parenting or behavioural difficulties. In Chapter 10, I mentioned that although pushy parents exist, they are rare. Similarly, parents who are utterly unable to control their child are equally rare – in most cases, they're the ones who have placed their child at the centre of the family and allowed them to rule the roost.

As for behavioural difficulties, unless the child is presenting this way both at home and at school, this is unlikely to be the issue. It bears repeating what we said at the start of the book: if you're not qualified to do so, making judgements about a child based on observation, let alone sharing them with parents, is unprofessional and even dangerous. If you have concerns as a teacher, raise them with your SENCO or Educational Psychologist and provide evidence.

If the child is well-behaved at home, it's equally common for parents to assume that the problem must be something to do with how the school functions or that the teacher must be unable to control their class, which are not helpful preconceptions. So, what is the answer? As I said, this is a recent trend and the facts lie within some yet-to-be-undertaken research before we can say for sure, but I suspect there may be several possible causes:

- Sensory sensitivities make the classroom an overwhelming place, and the child simply cannot cope.

- The child is used to being the centre of attention, and this is no longer so.

- The child had a false expectation of what school would be, and is now disillusioned and upset.

It's common for schools to be put on the back foot when faced with a professional report informing them that they have a gifted child in their midst. If you've never come across such a child before, and have only learned about them from the media, it's an understandable response, especially when parents assume educators must be intimately familiar with gifted children and how to deal with them. The report is intended to help but it can cause confusion and conflict.

The good news is that provision for Gifted and Talented (or More/Most Able Students, as they are sometimes referred to) in school can be straightforward, inexpensive and not particularly time-consuming. Your school undoubtedly already has a Special Educational Needs policy and a Local Offer (informing families what nearby support services are available) in place.

Adding a Gifted and Talented policy is much less work – I have one that I helped to write and would be happy to provide any school with the template. I've found that parents are far more supportive when there's a concrete plan in place, and a Gifted and Talented policy is a good start, so long as the school is able to abide by it.

Another parent-pleaser is the Individual Plan. Working together, parents and teacher put together a set of objectives each term where both parties play their part in helping the bright spark make progress and reach their potential. It's important that the plan works on both the child's strengths and deficits. Let's return to Ella, and look at two Individual Plans that her parents and teachers might draw up for her – one for when she's 6, and one for when she's 12:

Individual plan

Child's Name/Age	Ella (01/01/2007) Aged 6		
Date of Plan:	Summer Term 2019		
Area of Focus	**Action**	**Expected Progress**	**Responsibility**
Ella struggles to make friends.	1. School will have organised playground games that Ella will first of all watch and learn the rules for. 2. Parents will look at Family Mensa and other events that are suitable for Ella.	1. Ella will begin to take part in organised games in the playground. 2. Ella will attend some Family Mensa activities so that she can meet other bright sparks.	1. School 2. Home
Ella needs help to dress herself after PE.	1. Parents will work with Ella on dressing herself. 2. School will instigate an "I dress myself" certificate for each KS1 child that achieves this.	Ella will be able to dress herself without help by the next school meeting and will have achieved her certificate.	Home and school.
Ella's literacy and numeracy skills are at least two years ahead of her actual age.	Ella will work with the Year 3 class for English and Maths lessons.	Ella will work at a level that reflects her potential in English and Maths.	School.

Date of next meeting:	
Outcomes:	

Individual plan			
Child's Name/Age	Ella (01/01/2007) Aged 12		
Date of Plan:	Summer Term 2019		
Area of Focus	**Action**	**Expected Progress**	**Responsibility**
Ella is taking most of the evening to finish her homework because she thinks it's not good enough. This has meant missing bedtimes and clashing with her parents.	Ella will spend no more than 30 minutes on each piece of homework set. It will then be handed in regardless of its state.	Ella will get used to being more focused and producing 'good enough' work, allowing for a good work/rest balance.	Ella, with support from home and backed up by school.
Ella has not been eating lunch during her lunch break as she wants to practise for end of term concert. This has meant she's become listless and irritable.	School will arrange with the canteen for all students taking part in the concert to collect a packed lunch.	Ella's mood and performance in the afternoons should improve.	Ella, with support from the school.
Ella is a gifted mathematician.	Ella will join Year 10 GCSE Maths classes. This will mean she will have to catch up on work missed in her own time.	Ella will take GCSE Mathematics two years early.	Ella, with support from home and school.

Date of next meeting:	
Outcomes:	

Putting these measures into place is not an onerous task, but it works wonders for communication and good relations between home and school.

If you're a parent, complete an Individual Plan for your child using the templates provided for Ella. If you're a teacher, complete one for an exceptionally able child in your class. (You can find a blank version on page 125.)

Supporting a Bright Spark's Education in the Classroom

Hopefully, if you're a teacher reading this book, you'll now have a deeper understanding of exceptionally able children (and their parents). Although we've covered many of the behavioural traits that children with a high IQ tend to manifest, there are a few specific to the classroom that can be useful indicators you've a bright spark among your ranks:

- A developed sense of humour that may be mature beyond their years, inappropriate or odd.

- They're a compulsive communicator, and if you can't listen they'll tell someone else.

- They have an inability to sit still and will fidget, doodle and play with paper.

- They're a good multi-tasker and are paying attention even if they don't seem to be.

- They have poor handwriting, as their hand is unable to keep up with their brain.

- They're a leader rather than a follower and hate to be one of the crowd.

- They do well in tests (thanks to an excellent memory) but classwork is less impressive.

- They question everything and everyone, including the teacher.

- They have unusual hobbies or interests and will demonstrate vast knowledge of them.

- They hate to be wrong and will refuse to participate rather than risk failure.

- They find it difficult to make friends and their friendship group will be small.

If you suspect you have a gifted child in your class, there are some IQ tests that can be administered by qualified teachers or your SENCO. Parents, particularly those who had a poor education themselves, might not have picked up that they have a bright spark in the house. As we touched upon at the start of the book, though, don't assume that it's your most motivated, hardest-working children that are the brightest. It can be common for teachers to overlook gifted individuals because they don't present themselves in the ways you might expect.

When I run my workshops, I'm dealing with children from all over the country who go to different schools and have received varying forms of education. I cannot make assumptions about what they know, particularly when dealing with younger children, only that they are exceptionally able. My favourite way of working with them is to use open-ended tasks.

Open-ended working is a technique I started to favour when my son had started school and I took up some supply teaching to prevent my brain wasting away from being in the house all day. When you walk into an unknown classroom filled with unknown children it's a sure-fire way to engage them all. You set the scene, give the children their task and let them know how long they have to do it.

You might, for example, present a list of animals and encourage the children to find a matching fact about three or more of them using books or the Internet. Each child then brings as much or as little to the task as they're able and while they're self-occupied, you're free to move around, cajole, teach and support as needed. Any bright sparks, meanwhile, can fly free and may well polish off the entire list. Open-ended tasks aren't suitable for every subject, but there's very little they can't be adapted to.

In your own classroom, arrange a 'quiet study' spot where children who need to – for reasons of sensory sensitivities, autism or distress – can take time out. It's safer than having them leave the room to do so. An enclosed space that's away from windows, posters and loud colours is ideal if you can get creative with bookcases, partitions and other classroom furniture.

Have a pair of headphones in there to help block out noise and teach the children who need it to 'self-refer' themselves to that spot. Leave them be if they're in there – if they're overwhelmed or stressed, they don't need someone talking at them.

Finally, be mindful of the Four Rules for Success (see Chapter 9). Adhering to them, where you can, can help support what parents are (hopefully) doing with their bright spark at home. Remember, for example, that exceptionally able children need praising for their academic and in particular their interpersonal accomplishments just as much as any other child.

Managing Diverse Learning Groups

It's very common for schools to be dealing with a number of high-ability children at any one time, although they naturally tend to be scattered across form and year groups. This can make it trickier to accommodate their unique needs than if they were all in the same class, but it is possible. Schools have tried a number of different approaches over the years, although each has its own advantages and disadvantages. Let's summarise each:

1. Setting

Setting is where the children are sorted into sets for each subject based on their ability rather than their age, and the complexity of the work is scaled accordingly. In secondary schools, it's quite common that when a year group comes to a certain lesson, like maths or science, they separate out of their form groups and into classes that are working at a similar level of ability.

2. Vertical Grouping

Vertical Grouping goes even further and combines students from different year groups together into ability-based sets for most of their academic subjects – a primary school might mingle students from Years 1 to 3 together, for example, and the same with students from Years 4 to 6. A disadvantage of this approach is that it takes a huge amount of planning and organization to achieve, as you're asking the entire student body to split up, move around and recombine after each lesson.

Even though this approach may sound ideal for our bright sparks, they can still find themselves 'stuck' at the top of the top set as they get older. Additionally, the teaching staff need the flexibility and resources to cope with the whole school taking part in the same lesson at once. The main advantage is that it allows children to work at a level they find comfortable, but another is that older students in the group who might be working more slowly are able to see first-hand that they're more developed than the younger students in certain ways, and support them in a kind of 'big brother / big sister' relationship which helps improve their self-esteem.

3. Enrichment Activities

The third is to provide Enrichment Activities, prepared in advance, to stretch children who have completed the set work. A disadvantage here is that it's heavily reliant on an individual teacher to provide activities that strike the right balance. Less imaginative teachers either tend to provide 'more of the same', which our bright sparks will find boring having already mastered the concept, or work that's unrelated to what came before it.

One big advantage is that this extension work, if framed as a game or a puzzle, can be seen as a reward for the entire class to strive for. Alternatively, the high-fliers can help others in the class who are struggling, or you could simply provide a 'study box' and allow them to pick their own activity that interests them.

4. Differentiation

The fourth is to plan lessons around differentiation, so that students of all abilities have a work goal that raises expectations and helps everyone feel like they've achieved something. One common structure is 'Must – Should – Could'. 'Must' is work that's achievable by everyone, including the weakest child in the class, by the time the bell rings. 'Should' is work you would expect around half the class to complete, while 'Could' is extension work that half the class will make a start on but only one or two will complete.

A disadvantage here is that the teacher needs to prepare more work, and if the 'Must' material isn't levelled properly it means the less able students end up losing their breaks and lunchtimes to finish it. No fun for them! One advantage is that, if the 'could' work is deliberately set at a level that's borderline frustrating, attempting the tasks will help teach resilience and study skills as bright brains are made, uncharacteristically, to struggle.

5. Acceleration

A fifth approach is acceleration, where high-ability children are moved into classrooms with older students who are working at a level that challenges them, which is an obvious advantage. I was accelerated three years in my first primary school, having spent my first term in reception, my second in Year 1 and so on. I loved it, but that state of affairs only lasted until we moved house and I had to change schools. The physical disadvantages can be harder to overcome in lessons such as PE and art. Also, you have to wonder whether acceleration can be sustained indefinitely – is a child of 12 really prepared, socially and emotionally, to attend university?

When they're willing to be flexible, schools can cooperate to ensure there's provision for bright sparks. A few examples I've seen over the years are:

■ Children spend most of the day with their peers but join classes with older students for literacy and numeracy.

■ Primary and secondary schools work together to allow gifted primary students to attend maths or science classes at the secondary school.

■ Secondary school children might attend college or university lectures for a particular subject but stick to the normal timetable the rest of the week.

■ Local primary schools group together to run workshops for bright sparks, with each school taking its turn to host.

If parents, teachers and schools are willing to come together and think outside the box, the possibilities for providing a bright spark with a school life that both stretches and challenges them are many and varied, and no one needs to smash the production line to pieces in the process. Before that can happen, lines of positive communication need to be established, each party needs to assume good intent on all sides, and compromises must be reached.

It sounds daunting at first, but with a robust Gifted and Talented policy and Individual Plan that all sides, including the child, are willing and able to adhere to, school can remain the place it was always meant to be – a productive, contented experience that teaches valuable social skills. With help, our bright sparks can acclimatise to being a functional part of a larger group while still performing at their best. After all, that's what adulthood is all about.

Individual Plan

Child's Name / Age:	
Date of Plan:	

Area of Focus	Action	Expected Progress	Responsibility

Date of Next Meeting:	
Outcomes:	

Chapter 14

If it Ain't Broke...

Chapter 14:

If it Ain't Broke...

Throughout this book, I've returned repeatedly to conversations I've had with anxious parents of bright sparks and the concerns they've discussed with me. It's questions from caregivers like these that form the backbone of my talks, and – as we've seen – they can cover disruptive behaviour, school refusal, meltdowns, sensory sensitivities and more.

Before I conclude, I'd like to take a moment to consider one final common question I get, because I think it's just as important as all the others I've covered relating to physical development, social skills and education. Many times, parents have phoned me and asked something to the effect of "My child has just been IQ tested and come out in the top percentile – what should I be doing with them?"

Here's how I respond: if the child is happy at school and fulfilled by their class work, if they have a contented home life with friends and are developing into a well-rounded individual, if no issues are presenting themselves... then keep doing what you're doing! Your methods are obviously working. In the same way as I wouldn't expect most children to struggle with every single challenge I've mentioned in these pages, you might well have concluded that none of what I've discussed – be it problems making friends, trouble sleeping or coping with overthinking – is really a problem for your bright spark.

If so, fantastic! It may also be that while you recognise a few of the same tendencies I've talked about, in your child's case they were just a brief phase or you adopted a particular way of working through them that did the trick. I would encourage you to share those insights with other people. Affirming to fellow parents that the problems they're facing are neither insurmountable nor eternal can do wonders to help bolster the confidence of those currently travelling a rockier road than yours.

In times when things are going well, don't upset the applecart. The arrival of a psychologist's report or Mensa membership certificate in your home does not mean your child will spontaneously combust if you don't start feeding them 50 sums a day.

Also remember that however proud you are of your child's potential and accomplishments, most youngsters will not actively seek out the spotlight. Think twice before thrusting your child towards organised competitions or in front of a camera unless it's something they're actively seeking to participate in, and remember that their head still needs to fit through the bedroom door at the end of the day. Bandying phrases like 'my little genius' around won't help anyone in the long run.

Ultimately, when it comes to successfully raising a gifted child, almost all parents will get some parts right. Different families will breeze past some of the common hurdles and stumble at others. When difficulties do arise, remember that they are genuine difficulties with a real cause, and not just the result of a poor parenting choice or not trying hard enough.

Keeping the Four Rules for Success in mind, letting our bright sparks know that we're nearby if they need us and remembering to enjoy their childhood alongside them are just as important as how we tackle problems if they crop up. If all goes well, their natural intellect will provide our children with a huge wealth of opportunities to flourish and succeed throughout their childhood and into adulthood.

By facing challenges head-on when they present themselves, seeking support from others when we need it and encouraging resilience, we will get to enjoy watching a gifted child grow into a capable adult who's ready to take on the world. They may choose to do so as a superstar or a scholar; a bricklayer, bass guitarist or brain surgeon. Perhaps they'll pick another path we never even contemplated. Whatever happens, we will have provided the foundations for them to make that choice with confidence, and they will have learned not to be cowed by failure along the way. So long as we provide them with love and support, our square pegs can ultimately carve themselves holes that fit them very well indeed.

References

Bowlby, J. (1988) *A Secure Base: Parent-child attachment and healthy human development.* New York, NY: Basic Books.

Duncan, S., Goodwin. C., Haase. J., and Wilson. S. *Neuroscience of Giftedness: Greater Sensory Sensitivity.* Gifted Research and Outreach.

Green, A., and Gilhooly, K. (2010) In Kaye, H. (Ed) *Cognitive Psychology,* Chapter 11. Maidenhead: The Open University.

Hastorf, A.H. (2016) *Lewis Terman's Longitudinal Study of the Intellectually Gifted: Early Research, Recent Investigations and the Future.* pp 3–7. Published online: 01 Jun 2016.

Her Majesty's Inspectorate. (1992) *The Education of Very Able Children in Maintained Schools: A review.* London: HMSO.

Hitch, G.J. (2010) In Kaye, H. (Ed) *Cognitive Psychology*, Chapter 5. Maidenhead: The Open University.

Jacobsen, M.–E. (1999) *Encountering the Gifted Again, for the First Time.* Talent Development Resources.

Naish, P. (2010) In Kaye, H. (Ed) *Cognitive Psychology*, Chapter 2. Maidenhead: The Open University.

Ness, H. (2010) In Kaye, H. (Ed) *Cognitive Psychology*, Chapter 16. Maidenhead: The Open University.

Terman, L. M. and Oden, M.H., and Bayley, N. (1947) *The Gifted Child Grows Up: Twenty-five years' follow-up of a superior group. Genetic Studies of Genius, Volume 4.* Stanford, CA: Stanford University Press.

Terman, L. M. and Oden, M.H., (1959) *The Gifted Group at Mid-Life: Thirty-five years' follow-up of the superior child. Genetic Studies of Genius, Volume 5.* Stanford, CA: Stanford University Press. Retrieved 2 June 2013.

Tobin, J.J., Wu, D. Y.H., and Davidson, D. H. (1989) 'Komatsudani: A Japanese preschool.' In, *Cultural Worlds of Early Childhood.* Woodhead, D., Faulker, D. and Littleton, K. (Eds). London: Routledge.

Winnicott, D.W. (2000) *The Child, the Family and the Outside World.* London: Penguin Books

Further Reading

Coombes, S. and Clarkson, S. (2017) *Hello Happy! An activity book for children who sometimes feel sad or angry*. London: Studio Press Books.

Fonseca, C. (2015) *Emotional Intensity in Gifted Students: Helping kids with explosive feelings*. Waco,TX: Prufrock Press Inc.

Leyden, S. (1985) *Helping the Child of Exceptional Ability*. Abingdon: Croom Helm Publications.

Madison, L. (2013) *The Feelings Book, The care and keeping of your emotions*. (2018) Middleton, WI: American Girl Publishing Inc.

Orloff, S. (2018) *The Empath's Survival Guide: Life strategies for sensitive people*. Louisville, CO: Sounds True.

Painter, F. (1984) *Living with a Gifted Child*. Chapter 3. London: Souvenir Press Ltd.

Sand, I. (2017) *Tools for Helpful Souls: Especially for highly sensitive people who provide help either on a professional or private level*. London: Jessica Kingsley Publishers.

Serebriakoff, V. (1988) *A Guide to Intelligence and Personality Testing*. Carnforth: The Parthenon Publishing Group.

Wedge, M. (posted 3rd May 2016) *'What Is a "Good Enough Mother"?'* Psychology Today.

Williams, J. (2015) *Understanding the Highly Sensitive Child: Seeing an overwhelming world through their eyes*. CreateSpace Independent Publishing Platform; 1 edition (28 Oct. 2015)

Contacts, Resources and Useful Websites

Contacts

Lyn Kendall

Lyn Kendall. M.Ed., Dip.Psychol., Adv.Dip.SEN & Inclusion., MBPsS (CBT C&A AAC)

Lead Consultant, Kendall Tuition. Gifted Child Consultant, British Mensa Ltd.

https://www.facebook.com/KendallTuition

Tweet: @LynKendall1

Jane Evans

Tweet@janeparenting2

Contact: janeevans61@hotmail.co.uk The Lasting Life Change Coach creating the change you crave. Childhood Anxiety & Parenting Media Expert, TEDxSpeaker & Author

Resources

The Happy Puzzle Company Ltd. PO Box 586, Elstree, Herts. WD6 3XY (https://www.happypuzzle.co.uk)

Marzollo, J. I Spy books. New York, NY: Scholastic.

Useful Websites

https://www.mensa.org.uk/

https://www.potentialplusuk.org/

Highly Sensitive, Gifted, not Disordered. An article on the website High Ability website: http://highability.org/911/high-sensitivity-gifted-adults-disorder/

Children and Families Act 2014, Part 3. http://www.legislation.gov.uk/ukpga/2014/6/contents/enacted

https://www.gov.uk/government/publications/young-persons-guide-to-the-children-and-families-act-2014

https://www.sengifted.org/post/overexcitability-and-the-gifted

https://www.researchgate.net/publication/316583403_Giftedness_and_Sensory_Processing_Sensitivity_A_Validation_Study_of_Two_Versions_of_the_Highly_Sensitive_Person_Scale

https://www.repurposedgenealogy.com/2016/06/01/the-gifted-brain-and-sensory-processing-disorder/

https://educationaladvancement.wordpress.com/2012/05/01/5-definitions-of-giftedness

https://www.zerotothree.org/resources/1371-when-is-the-brain-fully-developed